What they're saying about the series and the authors...

"The West Orange Chamber of Commerce is proud to be connected with Mike O'Keefe, Scott Girard and Marc Price of **Expert Business Advice**. Their dynamic presentations, intellectual wealth, and unique insight into small business have helped numerous Chamber members take their businesses to the next level."

Krista Compton Carter, IOM

West Orange Chamber of Commerce Vice President

"Over the years, Scott Girard has provided my business and me with invaluable guidance and direction. He is a true visionary."

David Van Beekum, Owner

DB Tech Design, Inc.

"I've had the pleasure of working with Michael O'Keefe on many projects over the years. His ability to evaluate situations, identify competitive advantage opportunities and implement well thought-out strategic plans is second to none."

Jim Costello

Director of Project Management

Marriott International Design & Construction Management

"Marc Price is a business builder! I have seen him start with a blank piece of paper and create a million dollar business for a financial education online application and service. He is a natural network builder and relationship marketer who works hard, is very creative, and who usually surpasses all objectives for sales, service, and market share growth. You want Marc on your team if your goal is to grow your brand and increase top and bottom lines."

Mike Schiano, MA, CRHC, CPFC

Information and Technology Services

"As an entrepreneur and owner of Professional Accounting Services, I retained Mark Moon to handle complex tax and legal issues for my business. He consistently meets short deadlines with thoughtful counsel, keeping larger business objectives in mind and putting lesser issues in proper perspective. Mark understood our needs quickly and his advice has been very effective. His knowledge and broad range of experience in business, negotiations, and intellectual property allowed me to move forward, confident that I had the appropriate legal protection in place."

Anne Nymark
President, Professional Accounting Services

"Mark Moon has been an invaluable resource, from our first consultation prior to starting the business through the continuing advice and assistance he and his firm provide. Our business would not be where it is today without him. I strongly recommend him. "

Eugene Meisenheimer
CEO
Mocomei Services, Inc.

"Kate Scribner has worked and lived in a number of countries both as an employee and an entrepreneur. Her pragmatic, encouraging tips come from real-world experience and insight."

Lynn Collins
Talent Management Consultant in Europe
Global *Financial Times*-Ranked Leadership Solutions Company

INTERNATIONAL BUSINESS BASICS

INTERNATIONAL BUSINESS BASICS

Learn What You Need in Two Hours

Scott L. Girard, Jr., Michael F. O'Keefe,
Marc A. Price, Mark R. Moon, Esq. and Kate Scribner

Series Editor: Scott L. Girard, Jr.

A Crash Course for Entrepreneurs—From Expert Business Advice

Starting a Business

Sales and Marketing

Managing Your Business

Business Finance Basics

Business Law Basics

International Business Basics

Business Plan Basics

Time and Efficiency

Franchising

Social Media Basics

Web-Based Business

Supplemental Income

Distributed by Career Press, Inc., 220 West Parkway, Unit 12, Pompton Plains, NJ 07444, U.S.A., www.careerpress.com

D/2015/9797/1

Printed in the United States of America

20 19 18 17 16 15 14 13 12 11 10 9 8 7 6 5 4 3 2

Cover design: Bradford Foltz

Text design: Softwin

For all those international business pioneers out there—bridging gaps, connecting links, and keeping businesses competitive and ever-evolving.

Contents

Foreword

YOU CAN SPOT ENTREPRENEURS easily when they talk about their businesses and dreams. Their passion and fascination with their business—and others' businesses—is remarkable. When I met Scott, Mike and Marc, I knew before they told me about the many businesses they've collectively started that these were talented, insightful, seasoned entrepreneurs. We quickly agreed to develop the Crash Course for Entrepreneurs together. For this volume in the series, we invited Mark Moon to contribute his considerable legal expertise, as both entrepreneur and attorney, and Kate Scribner to add practical tips based on her years of international business.

The aim of this series is to give you high-level overviews of the critical things you need to know and do if you want to start (or you're already running) your own business. In a two-hour read. Of course, there's much more to know about every topic covered, but we believe that what you'll read here will give you the framework for learning the rest. A Resources section and a Glossary will ensure you can ground yourself in the essentials. And www.expertbusinessadvice. com, the co-authors' website, offers expanded support for entrepreneurs that is updated daily.

Entrepreneurs vary widely in their vision of international business. Your business may be large or small, and your interest in "going global" might be to outsource, buy parts or complete products, or offer your goods or services in a new market. In this book we try to give you information to think about and act on regardless of your particular goals. You will know how to adapt our advice to your own needs.

As we mentioned above, Mark Moon and Kate Scribner join Scott, Mike and Marc as co-authors for this volume. Marc Moon is a founding and the Managing Partner of the Moon Law Group, P.L., a full-service law firm. Over the years he has helped many start-ups and small businesses to make smart legal plans and decisions. Thanks to both his professional training and his day-to-day work with clients and managing the business of his firm, Mark fully understands the many, varied business issues any entrepreneur must face daily.

Kate Scribner has worked in international business development for decades in the human resources consulting and book publishing industries. She has seen things from both an employee's and an entrepreneur's perspective, and has worked, traveled and lived abroad for many years. We think you'll find her contributions pithy, useful and encouraging.

The initials of each author are noted at the end of each section. Here's a brief word from each of them.

I remember when I fully understood what our series of books should accomplish. We had recently decided that we wanted to write a series of books for people only moderately familiar with entrepreneurship and business. Multitudes of books already exist on basic levels of business practices and procedures. We knew that writing another one of those books wouldn't really serve anyone or change anything, no matter how well written it was.

On the morning that I "got it," I was drinking coffee and reading the news; the television was on in the background. I glanced up and saw a commercial for a foreign language software program in which, instead of learning by simply repeating vocabulary, the student is culturally immersed in the language, holistically surrounded with concepts of all manner of things applicable to the subject. In short, they don't list facts and terms and call it teaching—they show the student a vast array of information, on a multitude of levels, allowing her to bathe in knowledge.

I knew then that instead of presenting a bunch of facts that we think you should know about international business, we should take a more holistic approach and help you immerse yourself in global business thinking. Our method is most effective if you read this book cover to cover, skipping nothing. If you reach a section and either think it doesn't address your needs, or you think you know everything there is to know about the subject, read it anyway. It'll only take a minute—that's why the sections are not lengthy. It will enlighten and organize your thinking, either way. You'll see important concepts woven through various discussions, as they holistically fit in.

If you're hoping to read a book and immediately become the world's greatest global businessperson, this book isn't for you. If your goal, however, is to quickly understand and feel familiar with the basics of international business development, as one of your first stepping stones to greatness, we believe that our book has no rival.

I sincerely hope that this book will not only increase your understanding of entrepreneurship and basic international business, but that it also gives you pleasure and satisfaction as you learn the key principles and language of business.

Scott L. Girard, Jr.

When we sat down and decided to take on the daunting task of writing a series of books for entrepreneurs and small business owners, I cringed. I thought, "How can we ever reduce our advice and experiences to writing? And how can we cover it all—can we fit it into a book?"

Either way, we decided to get started, so each of us began drafting sections related to our respective specialties and work experience. Only as the initiative continued did I discover a certain passion for sharing my advice in a personal way, trying to convey how it felt to go places, negotiate situations, and experience new things, both good and bad, in the course of doing business internationally.

I take the same approach with business as I did with competitive sailing with my father when I was a kid. It's all about constant adjustment. You don't just rig the boat and go. It's about looking around, reading the wind, and predicting shifts and changes before they happen—just like understanding the external forces that affect a business or industry. While doing so, you are constantly looking around at other boats, just like you'd do benchmarking against other competitors in business—analyzing their speed and angle and comparing it to your own. Most often, what gets a boat (or business) ahead isn't some significant advantage; it's the inches or degrees of adjustment and the teamwork that generates the results. If you can point just a little higher or generate just a little more boat speed, it can make all the difference in the world—just like in business. If the organization can run just a little bit more efficiently, demonstrate better teamwork, identify the out-in-front opportunities, and not "just kind of want it" but rather, do anything to win, it will be the most likely to succeed.

I hope that this book will capture your interest, provide valuable information, and share an interesting perspective into the world of international business.

Mike F. O'Keefe

Everyone has heard the phrase "Knowledge is Power." I would have it read "Information is Power," for a couple of reasons.

We live in an age of instant information about every facet of our lives. We can receive news, on-demand weather and traffic reports, sports scores, social media happenings, and stock market updates. And yet, we forget much of this information within moments of receiving it, as new reports and updates are constantly replacing the data we were just beginning to process.

Most generic information travels fast these days. On the other hand, some information is meant to stay with us for a while, if not forever. And with that in mind, Scott, Mike and I set out to write a series of books to deliver lasting, valid information for entrepreneurs and small business owners.

Our passion for success in business and in life lies behind every page we write. As life-long, serial entrepreneurs, we have always taken the approach of surrounding ourselves with information, ideas and viewpoints from countless sources to support our efforts in constructing our next project. That information, when reliable and trustworthy, can and will be used over and over for repeated success. So, in essence, information is power, when applied over time.

Our series of books represents the hard work, research and application of numerous business philosophies, ideas and viewpoints. You will find rock-solid information that can be applied now…and later. It's information that can be shared, and then referred to as a refresher down the road, if needed. Our goal was to deliver information and advice that is relevant, smart and timely. We hope these fresh, contemporary approaches to the fundamentals of business finance will get you, and keep you, at the top of your game.

The way forward begins here…

Marc A. Price

When Scott, Mike and Marc first approached me about writing this book, I was intrigued, but I admit I had some questions. Why me? How could anyone produce a two-hour read on international business basics?

While discussing the proposal with them and with some of my clients and peers, they reminded me why they choose to work with me and continue to recommend my firm to others. First, I have the unique business experience of being both an entrepreneur and an attorney. I started and operated businesses (and consulted with several attorneys!) before entering law school. Today, we tailor the legal services our firm offers in ways that eliminate the fears of small business owners and individuals. I know how they think; I've been there—and am a founder and managing partner today.

Also, I've had a lot of practice in explaining the law. We focus all of our consultations and ongoing representation on the premise of informed decision making by our clients. We educate our clients so that they may fully understand the legal and business ramifications of the decisions they make. This is an unusual practice, but it works. Many of my clients are amazed by the process and their long-term successes, including in global business expansions.

Finally, I run my law firm like a traditional small business. We focus on areas like customer service, efficiency of operations and long-term customer relations in addition to the traditional practice of law. I realized that these qualities uniquely position me to contribute to this book, especially where the laws in question are multinational.

My legal training at first made me hesitant to attempt to break down and simplify complex issues. You easily can pick a random paragraph from this book and expand it to 300 pages, with cases and legal citations. But the concept of a Crash Course for Entrepreneurs book appealed to me, with its goal of making its readers conversant with key terms and principles. The challenge of connecting with you, the reader, and sharing what are indeed complex concepts through everyday language and simple examples is familiar to me. It's what I try to do every day with my client consults. As I wrote, I kept recalling a favorite quote from Warren Buffet: "The business schools reward difficult complex behavior more than simple behavior, but simple behavior is more effective."

I have tried to write this book with all of these principles in mind and to lay out the most complex concepts simply and straightforwardly. I hope this book will give you the tools you need for the ultimate success in your business enterprises, no matter where in the world they lead you.

Mark R. Moon, Esq.

In my earliest days of doing international business, I got hooked by the fun and passion I felt in making deals across borders. You meet and work with people who are adventurers, dreamers, and hard-nosed negotiators. Strange and wonderful things happen along the way, and of course there are the scary and risky and threatening moments as well. If being an entrepreneur is a roller coaster ride, then being an international entrepreneur is a three-ring circus, full of color and noise and challenges on many fronts at the same time.

Over time I've learned that the most successful international entrepreneurs blend vision and discipline in achieving their goals. I've set myself the task here of sharing what has served them (and me) well, so you can hit the ground, anywhere, running. Do your homework, test your assumptions and goals, work your connections and know what you don't know. I hope my contributions here will spark "Aha!" moments and that you'll soon be hooked and on your way to success too.

Kate Scribner

We all hope this book supports the fire and drive you feel now as you think about going global or confront the realities of running your own business across borders and meeting its challenges day to day. We wish you success!

Kathe Grooms
Managing Director, Nova Vista Publishing

Introduction

INTERNATIONAL BUSINESS CAN INVOLVE opening a new market to sell into, or finding new vendors who can supply you with goods or services you need for your home market, or a mix of those activities. So you might actually do both, acting as buyer and seller abroad. Depending on where you are in the life of your business, the nature of your business and your business model, international business may represent a new phase, or it could be part of your initial start-up model.

Here are some scenarios:

- You think your goods or services will sell well in the target market, so you need to set up means to enter that market.

- Your current local vendors or human resources (employees, freelancers, etc.) may not be the best for your company's optimal success. They might be overloaded, expensive, too slow, lacking technical expertise or equipment, poorly located, or have other limitations that can be avoided or minimized by moving their functions abroad.

- The target market is pro-actively seeking inward investment and is offering incentives (tax relief, start-up assistance, etc.) to make it attractive for your business.

Regardless of where you find yourself today, we invite you to scale our advice to fit your picture. Your established, growing business might be best served by outside consultants and professionals who can dig up the data you need to make smart choices. Or your shoestring, ambitious little home-based company might really be better off if you get on a train or plane and do most of the groundwork yourself. Our aim is to make you aware of the things you'll need to consider in any case.

We decided early on that our book would not be a country-by-country guide for entrepreneurs eager to expand across borders. If you need that kind of information, you'll find it in print, online, at conferences and expos, and in chance conversations or planned meetings. Be alert to bias, out-of-date data (things are changing very fast in the developing economies), current events and so forth. Sniff out any flaws in the information you collect and weigh it carefully as you plan.

We authors are all American born and a lot of our business experience, both as employees working in international companies and as entrepreneurs developing global business, has had ties to the US. However, we've also lived and worked in a number of countries, made deals and created companies all over the world. So we wrote this book without reference to any particular home country or target country, to leave you the room to fill in those details yourself.

One of the greatest appeals of international business is seeing how much people can be different and yet the same, the world over. The stark contrasts, subtle nuances, moments of high comedy and drama, and of course the hope for success make it a very exciting aspect of an entrepreneur's life. So let's get started!

CHAPTER I

Getting Started

The Case for Going International

Your business, big or small, can absolutely thrive
as a global entity…if you do your research
and develop a rock-solid plan.

MOST ENTREPRENEURS UNDERSTAND THAT starting a new business can be an enormous undertaking. And after that, at least for a while, your goal may be merely to survive. The countless pitfalls and roadblocks entrepreneurs face when opening their doors for the first time are uniquely daunting, regardless of your skills, preparations or current market conditions. However, when the dust settles, the ultimate goal of every business, large or small, should be not only to survive but to actually *prosper*.

And that may be why you are thinking of going international now. Just as when you launched your company, this new, multifaceted development process will require exhaustive research, an organized approach, and a plan of attack that will raise your odds of future success abroad.

Follow the signs

It seems almost every business is entering or already playing in the global economy now. It's natural that you've begun to ask exactly how your small business can *prosper* via international growth. Of course, you have numerous questions and can see nearly infinite factors you will need to focus on. Let's look at a few initial questions to put your thoughts into perspective. You are probably asking:

- What indicators prompted me to think about international expansion?

- Am I (or are we) up for the challenge?

- Do I have the right people in place?

- Is this the right time? If so, how will I know?

- Where is the logical location for expansion?

- What are the costs involved?

- Is there an immediate need for my products or services elsewhere? *Or*: Are there suitable, reliable vendors or service providers out there that will make my business grow better or faster back home?

- Do my products or services adapt well in the international market-place? *Or*: Do the goods and services I plan to buy need adapting for my purposes back home?

- Where do I begin?

These questions are by no means the only ones you need to investigate. They're just the starters. However, your answers to them can set the stage for those in-depth discussions with your partners, investors and out-sourced personnel in determining the viability of this important next step in the evolution of your business.

Steps you don't want to side-step

The biggest question, one we are constantly asked by entrepreneurs when the subject of international expansion and growth is brought up, is "Where do I begin?" And it's for a good reason. Having that rock-solid plan of attack is vital to your success, and the research behind it is no less important. Although all of this will be broken down as you read further, the following five steps will help you get this exciting process pointed in the right direction and assist you in determining the proper timing, the best approach, and the necessary steps involved in taking your business to the next level.

1. **Know what you don't know.** We all like to think we know everything, but sadly this is never the case. Expanding into another country will carry an entirely new set of circumstances with it. Having qualified and professional people and organizations to help you navigate through the labyrinth of legal, accounting, real estate, logistic, economic, and cultural factors will be essential to your success.

2. **Determine the viability of your products or services on the international stage; vet your potential suppliers.** You may be selling record numbers of your products or services locally. You may get the highest marks for customer service in your hometown. You may even be the local market leader in your industry. But does it translate elsewhere? Will the same marketing and advertising approaches be effective outside of your current market? Alternatively, if you are go-

ing global in order to expand your supplier base, you'll need to apply all the questions you'd typically ask a prospective vendor back home. Either way, it may be necessary to work with local experts to be sure you're getting valid, reliable information.

3. **Research the best fit for your expansion.** Countless factors will present themselves when you begin researching potential locations for your initial expansion. Be mindful of aspects such as the economic stability of the surrounding region(s), currency exchange rates, the ease (or difficulty) of import/export requirements, language and cultural considerations, demographics, the actual need for your products or services, the already-present competitors for your potential customers, local laws and the legal elements attached, and overall costs to operate in the region. If you plan to buy goods or service abroad, you can add questions about the reputation of vendors, the infrastructure, safety testing and so forth. Again, there are many other things to consider, but these elements will help shape the discussions regarding this particular step.

4. **Fire up that biz plan.** An absolute necessity for every entrepreneur, a fully-executed business plan is essential for putting everything into perspective for your future international growth. It will serve as a road map for your success; and it will demonstrate to investors, lenders, landlords and others your well-thought-out intentions and plans for your new a new market or source.

5. **Bring in others to help you get "in the know."** Every market and source of supply is unique, and often they can vary greatly, even over very short distances. Assembling a resource team of professional entities (legal, accounting, etc.) as well as locally-based individuals (residents, local businesspeople, agents or consultants, new referral sources, etc.) will help you understand everything from buying trends to cultural and economic aspects of operating a business abroad. Joining local business guilds and getting involved with several networking organizations in advance of your expansion will also help ensure success.

Make the case

In addition to expanding your flourishing business, crossing the threshold into an overseas market can help stimulate a sluggish or even stagnant enterprise. Working in new surroundings, experiencing a different culture, and discovering an untapped market or source of things you need can inspire you to take your business to even greater heights back home.

The case for going international should be one that stirs excitement and anticipation for you, your partners and your investors alike. Keep in mind that even though there will be pitfalls and challenges, a well-executed launch, based on proper research and a rock-solid plan of attack, can yield a sound and profitable business decision for everyone involved.

M.P.

How to Do Your Homework, and Who Can Help

*Homework, research, and analyzing every facet
of your expanded new business abroad is the
key to surviving… then succeeding.*

IT'S NOT GLAMOROUS. IT'S DOESN'T MAKE YOU ANY MONEY at the time. It's time-consuming and often complex. But doing the necessary groundwork, and then laying the proper foundation for your expansion efforts, is absolutely vital for surviving and succeeding in a new market abroad.

Of course, the official starting point of expanding your business internationally begins with a plan. And that plan is the fruit of extensive groundwork: the preliminary fact-finding that you do, the results of which you then organize as the basis for your expansion plan. This initial step sets up all the other elements of your expansion that will be used to measure its viability. Once your groundwork is complete, and your findings are validated, you'll have your rock-solid foundation for success.

Laying down your groundwork

Every aspect of your *current* local business gives you a template for your groundwork in preparing for expansion abroad.

Think about that business. There are certain features that you routinely analyze, review and adjust for its optimal performance. These features include, among others:

- The financial status of your company

- The current (and estimated future) status of the economy

- The line of products and services you offer

- Pricing structures

- Sales, marketing and potential growth strategies

- The performance and price/quality ranking of your vendors

- The opinions and viewpoints of your investors

- Expenses, revenues and taxable events

- Shipping, receiving, inventories and returns

- Customer service

- Competitors in the marketplace

- Market and consumer trends

All of these features will (eventually) be present in your target country if you are going there to sell or buy, and need consideration or projection when you expand internationally. And if your target market happens to be halfway around the world, there will be additional features to examine. You'll need to address them to determine if your business can establish traction in the target region. When you have acceptable answers or estimates for these items, then your next level of groundwork can start.

Go deeper

Your findings will help you to begin focusing on a certain region (or a small number of them). Then, you can ascertain their viability for the products and services you plan to offer or buy. The findings may indicate that things will be very similar to your original location or to others you are already present in.

However, the findings may point to vastly different offerings due to consumer needs, cultural aspects, pricing or other factors. If so, and if you feel the rewards are worth it, you'll need to dig deeper, and do more comprehensive groundwork before you move forward. At this point you should work out rough timetables showing how long it may take to accomplish this work (or when it is feasible to implement a stage). A partial list of those research undertakings includes:

- Seeking out the best location(s) for success

- Uncovering the best product sources or vendors, or discovering the best means of selling

- Learning and understanding the specific marketplace

- Grasping the local culture and respecting it

- Establishing an image and a presence

- Finding customers or specific vendors

- Determining the type of initial marketing/advertising you'll need to do, or what it will take to establish strong relationships with the vendors you've discovered

Immerse yourself locally

Ideally, you've been performing Internet searches, reading trade publications and attending trade shows and related events in your target market. Actually traveling to those locations will be useful; do so if possible, as part of your initial groundwork.

Such scouting visits can be an invaluable means of making that final decision in moving forward (or not) to the place(s) in question. In fact, for some, it's a mandatory step. But this particular phase of your groundwork can also be an adventure and a lot of fun. Immersing yourself in the local scene can unearth countless factors that research can't provide. You can much more easily answer varied but important questions like these:

- Do weather patterns or cultural traditions influence the market?

- What time do shops have the most foot-traffic?

- What is transport or parking (or other infrastructure) like in the area I am considering?

- Are local or regional politics going to be a factor for my business?

- Who are the key players (suppliers, competitors and such) I need to consider?

You can relatively easily come up with a hundred or so questions like these to tailor your research further. It all helps lay the proper foundation for future success.

Even simple people-watching can provide incredible insights into how you may want actually do business in a particular place.

- How do people interact with each other on a busy day?

- Where do they gather after a day of work?

- How many different cultures are represented?

- How many languages are spoken?

- What local trends am I noticing (fashion, food types, etc.)?

These sorts of questions can add real human dimensions to the data you've already uncovered. Their answers can provide unique perspectives that can give you a substantial edge when launching in an area that's unfamiliar to you.

And if you've had some experience in international expansion already, you may know that even a neighboring, seemingly very similar culture will have its particular quirks and customs. It can pay off well if you try to research such places with the same care you'd give to an "exotic" prospective market so you really can identify the nuances and work with them productively.

Help... please!

One of the single biggest downfalls of entrepreneurs is their reluctance to ask for help. Maybe it's a pride thing. Maybe most of us feel as if we know the answers or can get them without assistance. Truth-be-told, the answers to those vital questions can often be answered by local contacts (sometimes even entrepreneurs in the immediate area) who have a direct history and association with the location you are investigating. Many people can give you a head start on the groundwork you need to do if you simply ask good questions. And a long-time resident or shop owner's local perspective can deliver straightforward information that you could not obtain otherwise. Additionally, local governments, visitor and tourism bureaus, business guilds, trade or other associations, the press and similar resources can also supplement your overall research to help paint a comprehensive picture for your expansion plans. So don't be shy, and don't be too proud to reach out. It's part of the fun of international business.

M.P.

Market Research and Data Collection

Doing your homework, through extensive research and analysis, is essential in laying the proper foundation for your expansion to new markets.

IT'S PROBABLY SAFE TO SAY that most of us hated homework as school kids. It took a lot of time away from other enjoyable activities and seemed tedious and unnecessary at times. Today, as an entrepreneur researching a new market abroad, you may feel like you've traveled back in time, doing your homework. Performing endless research, analyzing data, following up on inquiries, and then evaluating the information once again can seem tedious at times. But the result of this exhaustive process should garner invaluable facts, figures and market trends you'll need to know when devising your international growth plans. And hopefully you'll also have some eureka moments, when you discover something exciting and promising for your business.

Understand the terms and their importance

If *market research* is a relatively new activity for you, don't worry, just get started. It's basically a well-planned process to help you assemble a working picture of specific target markets and/or the consumers or vendors within those markets that matter to you. The amalgamation and then analysis of that information can then help you assess the likelihood of your products and services succeeding there.

In your *data collection,* you will probably use multiple sources (interviews, email, phone calls, surveys, questionnaires, the business press, online information, etc.). Those sources can deliver either *quantitative* research (numbers or quantities) or *qualitative* forms (impressions, interpretations or images, rather than numbers). Assuming you are tapping reliable sources, you can digest and analyze the results to fill in more and more areas of your map of the local business landscape.

Why is all of this necessary? Think about it a minute: You're quite possibly talking about doing business halfway around the globe, in a culture, language and business world you may know little about today. Unforeseen obstacles could be waiting in the wings. You can't expect to know what you need to know about a new target market unless you do the proper research and analysis. Everything, from logistics to location and from market trends to demographics, needs thorough investigation to ensure your international business plans are on the right track. Investors and banks alike will want to review your findings in the form of reports, charts, graphs and narratives within your business plan as well.

Formulate questions… then go get those answers

Let's quickly assemble a few key questions to demonstrate how vital your homework is regarding your target market, assuming for the moment you sell products. If you sell services, or if your target market is going to be a source of supply or an outsource location, you can adapt the questions and add others accordingly.

- What are the current market conditions for my products there?
- How do the current (and projected) demographics correlate to my products?
- Do I need to have a physical presence? If so, where should I locate?
- What does the real estate market look like and how much will I have to pay to operate in the areas I am considering?
- What are the transportation options in these locations?
- How far will a customer be willing to travel to my business?
- What do the employment and earnings numbers look like in the region?
- Can I find quality employees in the locations I'm considering?
- What are the logistics involved in filling orders and receiving or sending shipments from the location(s)?
- Is this market considered on the up-turn or is it on a downward trend?
- Will cultural adaptation or translation be necessary, and affordable?
- What is the lead time from first commitment to first income and then break-even?
- What's the situation regarding payments? Corruption? Connections?

These questions will probably trigger more that you'll think of as you do your homework. Think of them as a small sampling of what will you will need to investigate before you can formulate a proper business plan.

Key areas to research to get the ball rolling

Let's also take a minute and list just a few segments of concentration (in no specific order of importance) that, without being overwhelming, can get you started on determining the practicality of your expansion to a specific region:

- The political climate, local laws and governing bodies and their possible effects

- Import and/or export opportunities and roadblocks

- Projected construction or development projects in the area

- Banking and finance infrastructures

- Current competitors and their success/failure rate in the area

- The presence of counterfeit goods or piracy

- Possible patent, trademark, licensing and other product safeguards

Drill down using SWOT analysis

The purpose of a SWOT analysis is to help you build powerful business strategies by ensuring you identify the key **S**trengths, **W**eaknesses, **O**pportunities and **T**hreats your business possesses or faces regarding the target market.

The first two components, strengths and weaknesses, are internally measured (e.g., company reputation, location(s), patents, etc.). You can influence them, altering and restructuring them when necessary. The other two, opportunities and threats, are external in nature (laws, competitors, environmental concerns), and are mostly elements you cannot control. All of these elements can make or break your success, and therefore it pays to know which things you can change, and which you'll need to adapt to, in your target market.

Just as we all learned as kids, the better you do your homework, the better chance you have to get good mark and positive results. As an entrepreneur, being prepared through research, analysis and in every possible way is not just a good way of initiating your international expansion plans… but the *only* way.

M.P.

What Model Works for Me?

Do-it-yourself solutions are not always the smartest.

WHEN EXPANDING INTO INTERNATIONAL MARKETS, often it's difficult to know which types of relationships or business models even exist abroad, much less what types are best for you and your organization.

Some entrepreneurs just assume that if you are entering a new market you must make the necessary time and capital investments to set up infrastructure, hire employees, research local regulations and perform the necessary steps and filings to make it legal for you to do business. However, there are many other ways to get your product or services into international markets.

Don't make it harder than it has to be

As we've been seeing, the first step in this process is to identify your target market and to understand how much potential business exists for your organization within it. During this process you may find that the total potential does not exceed the cost of creating a local presence for your company. However, as you do your research, you may discover that there are companies currently operating in your target market that will deliver a much better result and at a much lower cost to you.

It's funny, but sometimes working with a specialist in a particular geographical area or specialty can generate an ROI greater than you could generate without their assistance, and at a lower cost. It doesn't mean that you or your company isn't good at something or that you are missing the mark. Rather, it might be a sign of realistic business planning and unbiased, open-minded analysis.

Think about it for a second: Why do Fortune 500 companies often use third-party advertising agencies for various locations around the world? Why do manufacturers of products sell distribution rights and use independent sales reps in lieu of creating their own sales organizations? Or why do companies that source parts or complete manufacturing processes abroad use brokers or reps, rather than opening their own plants or trying to place a colleague in the country? The answer is simple. Often the third party has certain sustainable advantages due to their niche focus and local savvy.

For instance, a distributor of medical devices in Europe will already have developed a network of local and regional sales representatives, all with existing customer relationships. Also, that same product distributor probably has a clear understanding of European Union requirements ranging from required filings, approval steps, to label requirements, etc. It will take you a long time and lots of work to get up to that kind of speed.

So if you are a non-European manufacturer of a particular medical device, would it be easier for you to research *all* of these things yourself, making trips back and forth, spending a fortune along the way, only to finally be able to start the sales process from scratch without any leads, contacts or relationships, six to eighteen months later? Or would you rather invest time and money to find a reputable distributor who can handle everything and start selling your product in the new market with some reasonable volume in a shorter time, while you continue to run your business at home?

Yes, you may not make as much gross profit as you would working without a distributor. Yes, you may have to give up 20 per cent or 30 per cent in commissions. But, if you get 300 per cent more sales… more quickly… then… well, you do the math. Let's look at the primary types of relationships you might consider.

Partnerships

In this set-up, the parties entering into the partnership all agree to bring something to the table, whether that is capital, infrastructure, relationships and/or other resources. These are probably the most integrated types of relationships and business structures. Often partnerships share in expenses, labor and management resources and in the profitability of the organization. However, this type of business structure tends to be the most complex to initially set up and operate. Also, partnerships require more cash capital and human capital resources to operate effectively.

Joint ventures (JVs) and strategic alliances

These can be great because they can leverage the resources of the various participants. There probably are organizations that specialize in different elements of your business process (or extend beyond it) that your company doesn't currently have in place. Imagine sophisticated distribution experts, sales organizations, material sources, customer service resources, or intellectual properties that tie in with your product or service and can expand your revenue if properly set up. Or maybe your partners can expand your existing customer base or supply contracts.

We have a similar relationship established for our US-based medical device manufacturing business. We have developed some unique materials and a few patented designs, so we established a strategic alliance with a manufacturer of similar products in Australia. Our Australian counterparts then came to the United States, where we showed their personnel how to work with the new materials and how to make the designs that we developed. Now they not only buy the materials from us, but they also pay a small royalty to our organization for every product they manufacture and sell that is based on one of our designs.

In this example, we both benefited from multiple elements of the business process. We are able to leverage their manufacturing capability, skillsets and customer base to get our product designs recognized in an area of the world where we don't currently operate. For their part, they benefited from access to our intellectual property, cutting-edge materials and skills training. When these forms of partnership work, it's clearly a win-win enterprise.

Franchising

Franchising is another great model, for both franchisees and franchisors. The benefits vary, depending on which side of the equation you're on. If you have a knack for business and you possess the necessary skillsets and know-how, and you just want to jump into a fast-growing trend or business, then a franchise can be a great fit.

The franchisor is an organization that should provide almost everything you need to get started. This typically includes a handbook on how to run the business, financial modeling, marketing pieces, national marketing support, an established supply chain for products or goods, plus constant support, training and oversight.

In exchange, as a franchisee you pay an upfront franchise fee and ongoing royalties that average about 6 per cent of gross revenues. Your job is to select a great location within your territory, negotiate lease agreements, hire your labor and manage your business. Thanks to the franchisor's strengths, this can be a great alternative to spending a great deal of time and money in an attempt to create something new in a foreign market. The same cautions about doing your homework diligently and gaining the most favorable terms possible apply here, of course.

However, if you have created a successful business that could be replicated successfully by others, then it may be extremely lucrative for you and your team to put together a franchise package and model, and then find others who want to open additional locations in other parts of the country or world. This sort of business works best with such organizations as fast food restaurants or home service businesses (clothing repair and alterations, shoe and key shops, lawn care, child or pet care, etc.). Becoming a franchisor gives you the opportunity to generate additional revenues through your franchise fees, royalties and the ability to leverage the overall size of the organization to reach a broader audience in new market areas.

No matter what model you choose, just make sure that it fits with your vision of what you want to do as an entrepreneur and as a business owner.

M.O.

Making the Most of Others' Expertise: Agents, Brokers, Consultants and Reps

*It's silly to think you can or must do
all your international business
development yourself.*

ENTREPRENEURS EXCEL AT plunging into action and getting things done. They are also gifted (or get good at) recognizing when they can't do something themselves. For example, most know better than to do their own tax accounting or complex contract drafting. The same thinking can apply to setting up and running your business abroad, with added considerations.

Don't be discouraged or dismayed by the number of areas in which you may find outside help useful in your approach to a new market abroad. Many questions will be answered informally through networking, doing online research, perhaps visits to the target market, and so forth. Our aim here is to give you a heads up on how to identify and then close gaps, with the help of experts you identify as your research progresses.

Where do you need help?

Try this exercise to reveal where you and your team can do things yourselves, and where you may want to bring in experts:

1. Focus first on your business plan for the new territory. Ask yourself if you need any outside expertise in researching your target market so you can build a really solid plan. Can you get the data you need using only your current, local resources and information from the web? If not, make a list of areas where you need external resources to help with the process.

2. Sketch out a flow chart of a typical transaction in your proposed new market's business, noting for each stage whether you can handle it with your existing resources or where you need to use particular outside expertise (product development, sales and marketing, production, finance, legal matters, etc.).

3. Review the things you think you can handle with existing resources. Can they really stretch to work in the target market? Maybe they can, perhaps with additional personnel, training or supervision. But can they deliver results as fast or as well as people on site in the new locality? You may want to shift some internal tasks to external hands, or at least be open to that possibility. (It's fair to say that your internal people may gain more knowledge through trial and error, and feel more ownership and engagement in your new market's business, but that can be slow, expensive education as well.)

Now you have identified the types of expertise you should be looking for to support your expansion. It's rare that a business can expand internationally without some external support. At a minimum, if your home business is based in a multinational trade zone (like the European Union) and your expansion is within that zone, you probably will need to get briefed on cross-border taxation. Typically, entrepreneurs find they need at least to set up a banking relationship, find a legal advisor, and connect with people who can guide them through the business practices in their target market.

Typical areas where local expertise can help

As you saw from the exercise above, there may be many functions that might benefit from outside help to speed up your learning curve and ramp up business abroad with fewer delays and surprises. As we've noted, if your target market is nearby and quite similar culturally, financially and otherwise to your home base, you may find you need very little help. But as distance, both physical and otherwise, increases, the complexity increases even faster. Check your list from the exercise above against this one and add any functions you may have missed:

- Innovation and product development or adaptation
- Contacts and networking
- Customers and prospects
- Sales and marketing
- Language and customs
- Offices, factories and other real estate

- Labor, training, supervision

- Production—buyers, planners, quality and compliance monitors

- Logistics

- Law

- Finance—banks, investors, currency/payments in and out, taxes, subsidies

Who can help you?

If this is your first expansion to a new country, you may feel that there are far too many barriers standing in the way of expanding your business there. But countries and other entities recognize more and more that inward investment benefits their own people and economy, so they offer practical and financial incentives to attract incoming business development.

- Trade associations in your industry can help identify players to partner with (and also, identify competition)

- Global business consultants offer special services to help you gather data and make choices that qualify you for favorable tax, location, labor access and other supports

- Networking can reveal individuals or groups of sales representatives, brokers, consultants, retirees who want to keep active, freelancers and friends of friends who could provide you with important support, direction, and door-opening tips

- Government—both your home government and the target market's, at various levels—is not only there to regulate but to promote growth

- Special trade zones have experts on staff to help you with planning and making the most of their zone's special advantages

- Local legal affiliates, corresponding offices or trusted colleagues of your current legal and financial advisors—these contacts can be eyes and ears in the target market and help point you to further connections

- Sales representatives who might in future become external sales resources—they can be knowledgeable about local players, practices and trends in your sector (don't be naïve; test what you hear with other sources)

- Brokers who bring together suppliers and buyers—see more on this below

- Consultants—these can be former players in your sector, or firms set up specifically to guide newcomers through the mazes in the new market

- Contacts—you might come across someone from your sector who is between jobs and can help for a limited period of time, or a fellow entrepreneur who could make a good partner, or a freelancer who's happy to focus on one limited aspect of your business

Using a broker, agent or project coordinator

Your initial inclination to do things yourself and also to control start-up costs might make you think that paying a broker's fees to find suppliers, or screen candidates for roles in your new business, or whatever, is money you can save. But particularly when your target market is markedly different from your home base (e.g., your base is in Bolivia and the target is China), using a local broker or overall coordinator can make a lot of sense. For one thing, language and business practice issues you can't possibly master quickly are easily handled. Your broker can often negotiate better rates or pricing for the services or talent you need, and think up creative solutions to local obstacles to your progress. When problems do arise, a good broker can rely on the trust of the two parties she's brought together to work out win-win, face-saving solutions. Further, over time, you will learn a lot from a good broker as your business develops.

An agent is another potential external resource to consider if you deal in services or intellectual properties. Like a broker, an agent will charge a fee or a commission for the services provided. A good agent will study your offering and know who to sell it to (or create an acceptable license) for maximum benefit to you. Check who else the agent is currently representing (ask about past clients, and try to find out why they are now past, not current), ask who the agent sells to regularly, and make it clear how finances flow. You might want someone on the ground responsible for collections, from which commissions and taxes are deducted and then the net goes to you. Or you may want to show top-line income from abroad and then pay the commission and taxes directly. In some countries there's no choice available, but make sure you know the set-up before launching.

Plan for external resource and support costs

Don't neglect to budget for the costs of these services. They are part of your start-up and running expenses, and usually won't go away. Used wisely, external resources can give you funding, cut your costs, repay you in trouble and time saved, and free you to focus on the strategy and growth you are hoping to achieve abroad.

K.S.

International Business Do's and Don'ts

When travelling or working internationally, always remember that you're the guest. Be polite, professional and respectful, above all else.

DOING BUSINESS INTERNATIONALLY is very exciting. It can also be overwhelming. Not only do you have to bring your "A-Game" into play professionally, but you also have to work it culturally. It's just as hard to get it right personally as it is professionally. When one wrong word, hand gesture, or lack of action can deeply insult your overseas customer or partner, the stakes are insurmountably higher. You need to know what you're doing.

Before you travel abroad for business, it's smart to learn about that country's culture. Knowing the subtle rules about how to greet, or whether to make eye contact, bring a gift, compliment the food, ask about family or how the contact's business is going becomes extremely important. A misstep can sink a deal or relationship. For example, in German business culture, small talk is discouraged and business discussions should begin promptly on schedule. In contrast, in the Asian business culture, you are encouraged to respectfully build a relationship first, showing an interest in the other person. Only after you establish trust can you move on to business. These distinctions apply to timeliness of meetings, communication styles, subjects for discussions and negotiations.

While many international businesspeople understand that we all literally come from different places, in today's global marketplace, it's expected that new players have done their homework. If you plan to do business in another country, you must learn the basic do's and don'ts for that specific country. Don't assume that countries that are frequently lumped together under banners like Europe or Southeast Asia are similar. Spend some time on the Internet. Read up on your target country's customs and business culture. It may even be worth hiring a native cultural advisor, to guide or accompany you, if the stakes are high and have long-term implications. And if you are going to establish offices in another country, ensure your colleagues who will be in contact with or live in the target country receive their cultural education before they get into action.

The handshake

If you're from a country where handshakes are the norm for greetings, you probably feel that a good firm handshake says *I respect you, myself, our organizations and our future, and I've come to do some business.* However, in Japan, Saudi Arabia, and even France, it means something different.

Beyond that, what is your left hand doing while your right is shaking? Never thought about it? It matters. Bill Gates once shook hands with the President of South Korea and he absent-mindedly kept his left hand in his pocket—as he commonly does, because Gates *always* has his hands in his pockets. This seemingly insignificant detail landed him on the front page all over the world for committing a major greeting faux pas in his host country. Don't believe me? Google "Bill Gates handshake" and see what comes up.

Additionally, if you come from a handshake country, whether you're a man or woman, you'd automatically shake a businesswoman's hand, just as you would a man's, right? In fact, to neglect to do so would be rude or disrespectful, or both. However, in other places, you could cause yourself and your business some serious problems by shaking a woman's hand (especially if you're a man). The handshake is just one example, albeit critical, of how doing business internationally rests on attention to detail.

Here's a quick rundown to help you start your meeting right with the correct handshake:

- In the US or most of Western Europe: make solid, but not intense, eye contact; use your right hand, palm perpendicular to the ground; use a firm up-and-down motion two to four times. Don't look away, don't wink, don't shake like a limp fish, don't squeeze too hard, don't hold too long, and don't spit in your hand or slice your palm open with a knife first. The shake should project a tone of friendliness and respect, both solid and serious.

- Some places differ, however. For instance, in France, a single pump with a light grip is preferred.

- In the Middle East or Asia, a lighter grip is common, because a firmer grip can easily be mistaken as deliberately intimidating or aggressive. It's also common for businessmen *not* to shake hands with women. If in doubt, wait for the woman to initiate the handshake. If she doesn't, just play it safe and go with a light nod. Again, don't wink. In fact, never wink in business. Ever.

- In China, similar to Asia or the Middle East, keep the handshake light, and even hold on for a few seconds longer.

- Despite the adoption of handshakes in more and more countries, in southern Asia and elsewhere you may receive a Namaste greeting (it is also called Namaskar or Namaskaram). The greeter puts his palms together about chest-high, fingers pointing up and thumbs close to the chest. He may or may not say Namaste, which means "I bow to the divine in you," and makes a small bow. You do the same in return. Take cues from your counterparts and do as they do. However, if they bow, don't bow deeper than they do, as this could be perceived as disrespectful (that's in contrast to the bowing rules in Japan, where the junior person bows lower than the senior).

Kissing hello and goodbye in business

In most cultures where kissing is part of the greeting vocabulary, you won't need to worry about it in initial meetings. Once you've developed a more personal relationship with your contact, it may become appropriate (and in some cultures, this goes for men greeting men). The things to find out about kissing customs, if you get to that level, include:

- How many? Four is the max, to my knowledge, but there can be subtle rules about what the chosen number means (and surprisingly, in a three-kiss region, people who are related or very close friends may only deliver one, as a sign of relaxed comfort).

- Air or cheek? Some cultures favor air-kissing, while in others to do so, and not really connect, is considered stand-offish. If you are sick, you might say or gesture that you are ill and blow a kiss while staying safely at a distance.

- Touch while kissing? For people who come from non-kiss-greeting cultures, there's often a feeling that you should embrace or lightly hug the other person. But that can be read as far too intimate, especially in early kissing days. And generally, full body contact is not part of the deal.

- Which side first? Usually if you head the wrong way, and especially if you bump noses, people laugh and it's not important, but you might notice that there's a local pattern and you'll want to follow that.

- If kiss-greetings are new to you, it's very important to remember that if you have reached that level with someone, you do it without fail, both greeting and saying goodbye.

Your common sense will help guide you on when you reach the kissing stage (if ever) with your contacts, but learning the rules ahead of time will give you a lot of confidence and show that you respect local traditions.

Build language and cultural bridges

It may not be necessary for you to open an office abroad in order to do business there. If you work in manufacturing and/or outsourcing, however, it may be worth opening a very small office. That way a sourcing specialist from your home country can work alongside a sourcing specialist from the country in which the office is located. It's best when both of these people are bilingual, if two languages are involved. This way, they can work as a cultural fusion team to ensure all goes well between your company and the prospects, suppliers or customers in the country in which you're now doing business.

Dressing the part

I own several pairs of loud socks. Often, I elect not to wear a tie, but a two- or three-piece suit is standard for me. When I'm tie-less, I still want to inject color and creativity into my wardrobe. That's when I wear loud socks. Bright colors, shapes, designs—I even have a pair with many different-colored mustaches. Most people don't notice, but I typically get a smirk from the people who do.

Despite my pride and pleasure in wearing my loud socks, I would never wear them abroad. Why? Because many contacts would see my loud socks as a sign that I don't respect the culture, myself, or our business relationship. Yes, my socks would say all that. When in doubt, take the professional but conservative route, at least in your first meeting.

Learn at least the language basics

If you speak English, you start with a nice advantage in doing business around the world. People in many countries are multilingual, and more often than not, one of the "other" languages they speak is English. In fact, French was the universal business language for centuries. Now, it's being replaced by what's called "bad English"! But by and large it works.

If your target market speaks a language you do not know, you may not have time initially to learn it, but you really should learn the basic phrases. Memorize "yes", "no", "please", "thank you", "pleased to meet you," "my name is _____," "I'm sorry, I don't speak _____", "I look forward to working with you", and similar expressions. You might even write up a short paragraph of greeting and self-introduction, and then work with a native speaker to learn how to read it out loud with reasonable intelligibility. You can write it phonetically, and even if you have no clue about what sound means what, your hosts will be impressed (and probably amused) that you took the trouble to reach out to them.

Even if you, or they, provide an interpreter, it's a sign of professional courtesy to learn these few words. Doing so shows them that you respect your hosts' language and country, and if there's one thing that translates in all languages, it's respect.

It's impossible to over-emphasize the importance on doing your cultural homework on the country in which you're planning on doing business. You simply can't use what you might see as "common sense" to guess what's correct and not, and further, each country is unique when it comes to customs and courtesies. Cultural information is out there and easily accessible; when in doubt, just go the conservative route and take cues from your host.

S.G. and M.R.M.

Networking and Other Informal Resources

The most powerful tool in business also costs very little. Using it effectively and consistently will deliver tremendous results.

EVEN IF YOU HAVE USED IT TO FIND A JOB, build your local sales, or deliver much-needed information in the past, you might not think business networking can work for your international business development. But in fact, it can be the cornerstone for building your business abroad.

Business networking is basically building your business through others. It offers you an efficient, low-cost outreach system for developing business referrals, sales opportunities, industry contacts, and a steady customer base. If instead you are a buyer of goods or services abroad, it can give you industry intelligence (and gossip), connect you with vendors, let you vet their reputations, and so forth.

You can use networking to build your brand identity and help you quickly become a respected player in a new market. And it can be immediately effective for building, growing and succeeding in business, even abroad. That's because it lets you open or engage in discussions, form strategies, get referrals or references, and so forth, in the context of mutually beneficial business-building.

Just to be clear, I use "business networking" or "networking" here to mean face-to-face interactions that you get by attending meetings, gatherings and events; plus online or electronic means such as email, social media, and other similar sources. I don't mean the computer networks that link multiple computers together.

Network to build business on a strong foundation

Business-building should always be one of the main drivers of your business. Networking can give it a strong foundation. Your business abroad may thus be less vulnerable to external drivers like a weak economy, new competitors in the marketplace, or even a sudden shift in consumer demand. With a strong, broad, diversified network, you gain leverage by spreading your business-building efforts across a wide array of other entrepreneurs, businesses, associations and of course, the raving fans of your business.

So, where do you start? The good news is that wherever you turn, you can find a reason to interact with others to promote and support your growing enterprise. Let's take a look at the scores of possibilities available in the context of international business.

Face-to-face networking options

If you can spend time in your target market you have a wonderful opportunity to network fact-to-face with other people. Take a look at the list of networking resources on the next page. Many of these face-to-face methods are also used in job searches and information or fact-finding missions. As you review this list, begin thinking about how you can use the different resources to identify a good location, hire new employees, get referrals or references on vendors. You can use those resources for advertising, marketing and branding purposes, and for overall business-building. Of course, there are countless other options to consider, but this list should get your creativity going.

The Internet is smarter and faster than you are

I use this phrase often when training individuals and organizations in sales- and business-building. It carries even more weight when you are thinking of expanding internationally. Even if you're an extremely savvy and frequent user of the Internet for your business, it is still essential to remind yourself how vital a role it can play in laying groundwork and building that rock-solid foundation you want as a basis for your business expansion in your target market. It is indispensable as a networking tool.

Of course, the research component of your Internet activity will always be there. But it's the interactive side that you can take advantage of immediately and often, by going online and networking electronically, when face-to-face contacts may not be easily made. Give these online options a try:

- Join several national and/or international industry-related organizations

- Participate on online discussion boards and "chat" with other like-minded professionals

- Establish presence for your business through every social media channel that makes sense and that will ultimately generate results

Networking Resources

- Fellow entrepreneurs and local business owners in your sector
- Industry suppliers and vendors
- Chambers of Commerce or business guilds and associations
- Industry-related organizations
- Professional organizations (for doctors, dentists, attorneys, etc.)
- Local government and elected officials
- Schools and universities
- Fraternity/Sorority members
- Conferences, conventions, symposia
- Trade shows and exhibitions

- Volunteer organizations and activities
- Charitable organizations and activities
- Religious organizations and communities
- Staffing agencies and job-seeker outlets
- Elected officials
- Private social clubs (Elks, Rotary, Kiwanis, etc.)
- Local community events (festivals, markets, etc.)
- Athletic organizations (golf leagues, soccer or football clubs, etc.)
- Health and sport clubs
- Databases, directories, email lists
- Family, friends, neighbors, colleagues

- Find suppliers, vendors, fulfillment houses, employees and even future customers by interacting with them online and learning about their backgrounds, capabilities and/or needs

- Join blogs, news sites and other online resources as a contributor to tell everybody about your business and the industry in which you operate

- Gain credibility through all these channels and establish yourself as a legitimate expert in your industry by telling your story like a true business pro

These efforts will undoubtedly augment your face-to-face efforts, as well as help you reach a much broader audience to grow your business outside its local boundaries. You'll also gain an undeniable advantage and develop incredible insights about your target market and the industry sector in which you work, as it exists abroad. And you will begin to identify your potential and actual customers' needs or your prospective vendors' ways of working in the target market.

Make a plan and follow it

As with so many things in your life as an entrepreneur, you are free to do things spontaneously, or by plan. In networking you'll probably find a bit of both is best. If you bump into a stranger in an airport or lobby and discover mutual interests, exchange cards and follow up. Make sure you have your "elevator speech" (your two-minute or less description of what you do and where you're going) in top shape for the new market's needs. And on the planning side, evaluate which networking approaches could work best for you and set some measurable goals for acting on them in a defined period of time. The point is to seize opportunities and also follow a game plan for networking, so you can make sure to work every possible angle and resource for maximum success. Now, go forth and connect!

M.P.

Trade Fairs, Conferences and Other Events

Whether you are prospecting or maintaining important business connections, these occasions can help expand and support your work abroad.

PERHAPS YOU ARE USED TO ATTENDING OR EXHIBITING at the events where people in your business sector do business and gather new ideas and connections, whether locally, regionally or nationally. Or perhaps this is all new to you. Regardless of your level of experience, the magic key to making them productive comes down to three Ps: Prepare, Perform, and Produce. There are some special twists when you think in terms of international events.

Preparing

Suppose you think that maybe your product or service could sell well in a target country. Or you think maybe the labor, supply chains and other assets of another country could help you bring your product to market more successfully or profitably back home. Maybe it's time to hit the road and see what is possible, in person.

Through your home country's trade journals and associations, you should be able to identify gatherings that attract the organizations and people who could become your new customers or suppliers. These might be traditional trade shows with stands (booths), or tables, or suites in hotels where business gets done.

But there could be other venues for this kind of compressed market research. Maybe your field holds conferences where the latest thinking, innovations, or market trends are the centerpiece. Maybe academic symposia attract the people you need to talk to. In any case, talking to or corresponding with people who attend these events and asking them what events are key in your sector will point you to a few you should consider.

Don't be afraid to also contact the organizers of the events, understanding that they are likely to be viewing you as a prospective customer for future events. Filter what you hear and test the information you gather this way carefully. You are after answers to questions like these:

- How many exhibitors (or presenters, or companies, or experts) attended last year?

- Can I get a copy of the attendee list or the catalog of exhibitors?

- How many non-exhibitors attended as visitors?

- Do you put on special presentations apart from the expo side, to facilitate information sharing and networking?

- What sectors are represented?

- Is this a show-and-tell event, or are orders placed on the spot?

- Is this a national (or local/regional) event, or is it broader in scope?

- What services are provided for visitors? For exhibitors/presenters?

- Are there online data sources that will help me set appointments, etc.?

- What are the costs, and what is or is not covered by them?

- Does the event work with hotels nearby to get good room rates for attendees?

- Is there a special program for first-timers to help them make the most of the event?

- What support do the organizers offer for any logistics you'll need for display materials, set-up, take-down, or presentation technologies (like Wi-Fi, monitors or projectors)? What is the local electrical current and plug configuration?

- Will I need an interpreter or other local talent and labor to work effectively? What will they cost?

- Are there any tax or government incentive programs to encourage me to attend? (This could be provided by your own country, as well.)

- Can I recoup any taxes I pay to attend or exhibit?

- Are there any group stands or display spaces that are sponsored by my home country, region or particular sort of business that I could join for at least my first outing?

You should be able to articulate measurable results you hope to achieve from this adventure. Do you need to find two competitive vendors? Or identify three or more sales reps to handle your goods? Of course you are also attending to get the general lay of the land, but being clear about your goals can help you keep on track in the midst of the event.

Preparing also involves lining up as many contacts and making as many well-qualified appointments as you can ahead of time. The prior year's attendee list is invaluable here. Book appointments as far ahead as you can, and expect delayed replies (so be politely persistent if you don't get answers at first). After all, you are nobody until you connect with others.

Check to see if your local, regional or national government offers support or subsidies for your expansion abroad. See if there is a commercial attaché in your target market, and contact her well before the event to see if she can help identify local parties to meet with. Ask if the attaché plans to attend the event and set a meeting there, if so. If not, consider meeting her at her office. Making this connection sometimes really helps open local doors.

Do as much homework on the parties you will be meeting with as you can. This may involve a translator if their websites and trade news notices are not available in your language. Get your business card translated, and make sure you have visas, shots, maps, local currency and other basics covered. For some countries, your visa application may need to include an invitation to meet with someone, or a copy of your plane or hotel confirmation. Some countries only issue visas once you have arrived, and may only accept certain forms of payment (sometimes including only freshly printed cash notes!). So allow time and budget for these items as well.

Get your own kit together too. Pricing, schedules, specs, brochures, and whatnot may need time to develop and possibly translate before you go.

Think through the logistics as well. When do you need to ship materials you will need? Who's going to set things up and take them down? Do you need to arrange for someone to babysit your stand and goods if you plan to leave before the event is over? Can you store things onsite for the next year's show? When will you arrive and depart, and does that plan allow for local travel to the site, plus some kind of recovery from jet lag?

Performing

Seasoned businesspeople agree that foreign trade or professional events can be bewildering, exhausting, disappointing and worse. But they can also be great fun, and can open doors and build relationships in ways that long-distance contact just can't. They notice that even though an initial meeting or two might not produce orders or the resources you are looking for, they ease progress. And those personal contacts are even more valuable if you run into problems down the road.

Along with your agenda of meetings and events, bring whatever form of record-keeping devices you prefer, ranging from a pad of paper to two-part forms to a smart phone (and its camera) or a computer or tablet on which you summarize info to share back home. Collect the sales or data documents you'll be offered by contacts (if possible, request PDFs to be sent so you don't accumulate tons of paper). As you progress through your meetings and events, assign initial priorities to the leads and contacts you develop. You can always revise them as you learn more over time. If you can, complete a summary of each key contact and follow-up actions, right away, when the details are fresh.

Try to schedule time to walk the show or just schmooze with event participants and its management or sponsors. Sometimes those moments can lead to discoveries you'd have missed if you stick to your expo table.

It's essential to pace yourself. If you have business lunches and dinners every day and are working hard at the event all the rest of the time, you may burn out before the event ends. Particularly when the language, culture, food and climate are different from home, you can easily overextend yourself. If that limits what you accomplish, you've wasted time and money. On the bright side, if you can afford to stay a bit longer after the event is over, either to relax or do more market research, that can pay off in ways you may not recognize at the time.

Producing

To get the most from the investment you've made in this exercise, follow up rigorously. Prioritizing all your leads will ensure you focus on the prime ones first. Send out your specifications, quotes, samples, summaries, slides, pricing—whatever you must deliver—promptly. Confirm all the key points and highlight open ones in writing. Answer questions and requests for information by the deadline you promised, and so forth. Once you have dealt with everything in a first round of follow-ups, run through your summary sheets to point yourself to the best emerging prospects, and zoom in on them while the lesser quality leads simmer along. Plan regular reviews of your progress and don't waste time with weak opportunities.

In some cultures, you may find that your first year as an attendee or exhibitor is rather disappointing. Sometimes it takes showing up and participating a couple of times or more to prove you are "serious" and worth trusting. Still, you will be learning as you go along, and with time and clear focus, you'll know what your target market can provide for your company's future.

K.S.

Tech Tools to Shrink the Distance

*It's hard to imagine doing business globally without
some of the tools you'll learn about below.*

YEARS AGO, DOING BUSINESS INTERNATIONALLY was quite different. It required everything from telexes to translators to travel agents, not to mention a lot of time and money. Often overseas business meant getting on a plane, actually going to the target country, and meeting with people face to face to discuss... well, everything. Even the most basic communication tool of all, the phone, was very expensive and unreliable—in some places you had to book a call time in advance, via an operator. Yet despite the cost and inconvenience, old-time phones didn't give you any "face time".

Wow! Just look how far we've come in today's tech-savvy global marketplace! Now we can host virtual boardroom discussions and communicate with sight and sound, in real time, while sharing collaborative work files and presentations, streaming to and from all corners of the earth.

Keeping pace

Now that we have the pleasure of living and working in such a fast-moving and ever-evolving era, we have to learn to leverage all of the resources available to us to maximize our companies' progress. This is important for two reasons. First, it's an opportunity to save time and money and to maximize outputs and profits. Second, it's important to consider the competition at all times. Don't get consumed by focusing on what tools they are using. Rather, make sure that your company is staying relevant and moving along at the same speed, using the same or better tools than the competition. This will ensure that you won't be left on the side of the road.

When I think about international business and all of the different tools, resources, software, social media, etc. that can really propel a business forward, a few come to mind that have delivered exponential results in my businesses.

Social media

There are so many social media platforms available today, it's hard to choose which are most beneficial. In part, it depends on what you're doing. For example, a great networking platform for business in general is LinkedIn. It allows a user to search for contacts that may exist in their own personal contact lists; or search for individuals, persons with certain business titles, companies, specialty groups and even industries. Other platforms can be great in other ways, such as Instagram or Pinterest. These sites have been essential in sharing pictures of merchandise that retailers are trying to expose or to identify trends in a market segment. The list goes on and on, but social media platforms can be used to seek out new business, make connections within an industry or simply share a product or service with the world from a standard smart phone. The applications to your international business activities are obvious and endless.

Resource websites

In addition to social media platforms, there are plenty of websites dedicated to providing information, services and resources to business and entrepreneurs. One of the most popular is Alibaba, a leading web-based resource that specializes in connecting factories and other types of manufacturing reps with buyers from around the world. These relationships focus on everything from medical devices to toys and other consumer goods. And best of all, the participants on the site are all over the globe!

Aggregated email systems

These systems aren't exactly new, but they have proven to be one of the most useful and beneficial tools of the 21st century. By using an email aggregator such as Outlook or Apple Mail, a user can monitor multiple email accounts, reply from different accounts, create calendar events, set reminders and even create file folders that can be used to archive communication and documents for future access from anywhere in the world.

Dynamic video conferencing

This technology has been a game changer for international business in particular. These new systems allow for meetings, information sharing and collaboration to be done via live streaming connections which allow all of the participants to see, speak and interact with one another from anywhere in the world, as long as a fairly robust Internet connection can be found.

As with in-person meetings, the quality of these meetings rests on solid preparation, a clear agenda, strict start/stop times, focused discussion, and clear outcomes (regarding who does what by when in follow-ups). When time zones make it inconvenient for some attendees, it's courteous to "share the pain" and vary the time of regularly occurring meetings on a routine basis, so everybody eventually gets the joy of the 2 AM business review.

Email blast services

Snail mail is dead, and now it's often the most expensive type of marketing tool, relative to the sales conversion that typically comes with it. Now, for next to nothing, you can reach all of your customers and potential customers with the click of a mouse. The other great thing is that you get helpful data and tracking information, which help you to better understand who is opening your emails, when to send them and what type of click-through rate you achieved. As you build your international business, this tool becomes more and more important in letting you keep distant customers and prospects, as well as suppliers, up to date on your latest news.

Digital faxes and scans

Remember all of those old fax machines, the ones that would burn up reams of paper and black ink? Well, now you can send and receive your facsimile through your computer without using any additional resources. You can pick and choose what you would like to print, vs. having everything show up in the tray, whether you needed it or not! The same applies to documents that need to display signatures, like contracts. Scanning and emailing them saves courier fees, time and paper.

Virtual Private Networks (VPNs)

These have changed the way larger companies do business, more than ever. VPNs allow employees to log into a secure computer system from anywhere, giving them necessary access to pertinent documents and customer information. This has also provided a huge cost savings to companies with large employee bases, because of their ability to offer work-from-home opportunities. For a small company, the advantage for international business is the ability to log in from anywhere and securely pull up any data needed. No more lugging hard copies around the world.

Voice Over Internet Protocol (VOIP)

VOIP is another great way to communicate with individuals and businesses all over the world. It can support video, conference calls, messaging and call forwarding, too. Often it's available free of charge, or for a fraction of landline and mobile communication costs. And you can choose country or area codes, phone numbers and your call origin information. You can then put people receiving your calls at ease, by seeming to call from within their area. The only down side is that interruptions from weather, congested bandwidth and third-party maintenance may interfere with your scheduled events.

There are a lot of little tricks like these that not only reduce costs within your small business, but can make you and your business seem larger and more established than it really may be. It's unfortunate, but we live in a world where people form notions about a business or businessperson based on the way they communicate and conduct day-to-day business. Using some or all of these resources can greatly enhance your ability to succeed.

M.O.

Identifying Customer Trends with a Global Perspective

*Understanding and then identifying the significance
of your customers' behavior is critical to success.
And when certain trends begin to develop,
it's time to take action.*

REGARDLESS OF THE TYPE OF BUSINESS YOU OPERATE, every aspect of your operation, at some point, will point toward your customer. Customers' needs or wants put you in business. They also keep you in business, and this fact will never change. Keeping on top of constantly changing customer trends is critical to your success, both locally and abroad.

In this section we'll focus mostly on consumer trends. If your business is a B2B (business to business) enterprise, or if your international expansion is targeting new suppliers or outsourcing services, please feel free to "translate" the advice to your somewhat different circumstances. For you, trends within your industry, your customers' industries, and external conditions might be more important to monitor. But you will benefit from tracking consumer trends in your target market as well, since they may impact labor, manufacturing, finance and other major factors in your business abroad.

Understanding consumer behavior trends

Trends usually emerge when fundamental customer behaviors collide with outside changes to generate new wants or needs. A trend in consumer behavior develops when a pattern of behavior starts moving in a general direction, tracking a particular course. Think of baby booms, downsizing, home solar panels and the latest food fad. Recognizing these cause-and-effect factors can keep you ahead of the curve. Some trends are short-lived, others play out over generations.

Consumer behaviors and preferences can change swiftly and often, feeding an industry of trend-watchers.

In terms of your international business, you naturally will have to work a bit harder to monitor trends and identify the elements that could impact your business from some distance away. Even though it makes an already difficult task more complex, you still need to keep an eye on trends in your target markets. If you do, you won't be surprised by changing behaviors and can stay not only relevant but successful, long term.

Fact-finding resources

So, where do you start? Usually it begins with questions, and lots of them. It's just amazing to see the amount of information you can gather when you simply ask. And in order to get the ball rolling with your initial fact-finding mission, it's best to identify the easiest methods to acquire this vital information. Let's take a look at how this can be accomplished with little effort.

- **Learn from your current (and potential) customers.** You may be surprised at how willing customers are to share their opinions about experiences in your target market. Your personal network may have leads to resources and insights into trends that could be really valuable. So in your daily contacts, even in your home market, ask if your contact has any news, impressions, contacts or experiences about your target market (this assumes you don't mind them knowing you're thinking of launching a business or purchasing goods or services there).

- **Read the business press in and about your target market.** Here, you'll get the benefit of local analysis, background and forecasts. Most non-English speaking countries have an English language newspaper, and these often focus on issues and events that foreigners need to know about. Take a look also at the respected international magazines like *The Economist* or newspapers like *The Wall Street Journal* or *Financial Times*. They run features as well as news stories on business issues in all parts of the world. It goes without saying that you will need to keep an eye open for bias and propaganda in any information you discover.

- **Get active in social media and through online forums.** Learn what consumers in your target market are saying online as they share their opinions and preferences. While this kind of research is not filtered and definitely can be time consuming, it still may give you a broader perspective of what consumers are saying about specific products and services, including your potential competitors or vendors in the target market.

- **Talk to local shop owners and business organizations when you visit.** Introducing yourself to local entrepreneurs and getting involved with local business organizations can be invaluable when looking to understand the new market you are entering. Local customs, buying habits and other elements will play a huge role in your success. What trends do your contacts see that are relevant to your business there?

- **Read and observe… everything.** Read the local papers if you can. Visit shops and markets. Watch the local television ads. Listen to local talk radio programs. Take a look at the outdoor advertising: on public transport, billboards and train station posters. The messaging here will go a long way in describing what others are buying and interested in at any given moment.

Of course the information you gain from this research is only as good as the analysis you give it, so test out conclusions, keep an open mind, and keep adding to your pool of information as a regular part of your work on the target market. This foundation of information and feedback can be extremely eye-opening. It can also help you formulate a solid plan of attack even before you open your doors. Knowledge is the single most powerful tool you could ever have.

Trends… advanced

So, once you've done just about all you can personally, you can decide if that's adequate for this market. If the nature of your business is fairly straightforward, your research may be all you need to size up the scene and identify risks and opportunities. If, however, it's a complex business and involves a good deal of investment and perhaps a long period of time before pay-back starts, it might be good to expand your knowledge base.

You might be able to locate focused market research reports online via resources like ResearchandMarkets.com. Or bringing in a professional organization that specializes in identifying consumer trends and behaviors may be worth investigating. There are numerous international companies that can generate studies and reports specific to your needs as a business owner. These organizations can help you interpret the business climate and trends in your target market. Knowing the prospects and potential adversities that are present can save you time, money and reduce risk in the long run.

Most of these companies use the same avenues as discussed previously (surveys, etc.). However, a more in-depth look on a much larger scale will deliver additional clarity and understanding to your decision-making processes. Adding detailed research studies and delivering various sales forecasting models can also aid in defining your path to success. Be sure to check references before signing up for a project, just as you would with any new vendor.

Make sure to get it right

Regardless of the ways you go about determining what significant trends are operating and emerging in your target market, you will then need to apply what you've learned to your business models, asking whether your current ways of doing business at home will succeed abroad. That's why it is imperative to do your research homework before you launch. Learning by trial and error, in the dark, has low odds of success. But having a grasp of your target market's workings will give you the edge you need to be successful today and in the future.

M.P.

Facts and Rules

*Expanding your business in international
markets can be very exciting. Ensure
you know the right way to do it.*

IT'S AN EXCITING TIME to be in global business, but it can have its challenges. One of them is that each country or trade zone is governed by its own sets of regulations for conducting business, particularly when importing or exporting products. If you want to do business in another country, you must abide by its rules. Add in the mix of language, culture and geographical influences we all encounter abroad, and it's a heady cocktail to savor.

Mike O'Keefe and I started a US company a few years back that specialized in outsourcing small motors and related components, as well as large-volume lighting for hotel chains. China was known then for cheap labor in manufacturing, so we started and built our business there. We soon found out that only Chinese citizens can own businesses in China. It is a way for the Chinese government to ensure that the gross domestic product (money made in China) stays in China, in the form of Chinese taxes. We were only allowed to do business with Chinese factories and sourcing specialists in order to make our business work.

Starting out with solid facts and plans

When you start thinking about doing business outside your headquarter country, it's best to remember a few key tips.

- Doing business abroad will be unlike doing business at home. Don't take anything for granted.
- As we've said, read up about the target country in general, so you have a feel for current events, politics, trends and the economy, geography, history and culture, including its customs and courtesies.

- Educate yourself about your own industry sector in the target country via trade journals, online resources, your government's commercial attachés.

- Get reliable tax advice. For instance, if you are a US company, no matter where in the world you operate, you must still follow US regulations regarding compliance, financial and legal obligations. You must still pay US taxes, even for revenue from your offices outside the US, as long as you are a company incorporated within the US.

- With all your research complete, draw up a complete business plan and review it with a tax expert and a lawyer familiar with the target country. If your usual attorney is not versed in the area, he can recommend a qualified one.

Scoping out the target country

If you plan to send one of your employees or an official representative abroad to scout and develop business contacts, ensure you've done your homework on that person too.

- Will she project a professional, positive image of your company?

- Is she a flexible, resourceful, comfortable traveler?

- Does she speak languages that will be useful?

- Does she have proper travel documents, and have you checked visa requirements?

- Is she competent in her job function so she can develop contacts, interview prospects, collect information, get pricing, give specifications, etc. properly?

- Will she will behave ethically and responsibly while on the assignment? If you are a US company and she commits a crime or violates any business ethics laws while overseas and you didn't conduct your own background check on her, the US Department of Justice and the Securities and Exchange Commission (never mind the target country) could hold you and your business responsible for her violation.

Going global can be very exciting, but also very confusing, challenging and downright risky. The cost of consulting with an international business attorney and tax advisor will save countless headaches and is merely a fraction of what you could pay if you get into trouble. Stay on the safe side and let experts keep you prepared and advised.

S.G.

Working Through Your International Business Plan

*With this plan in hand you'll have a firm
foundation for business abroad.*

MANY OF THE STARTUPS or young businesses we meet with at our law firm
tell me they consider international business as something reserved for jet-set executives and Fortune 500 companies. However, they may be doing international
business without really knowing it.

Some of the most common, yet not highly visible, examples are entrepreneurs who order products directly from international suppliers, even if it is just
one component of the item they eventually sell. If it is supplied from across an
international border, then you are doing international business. Or perhaps you
have a retail business that offers online or catalog sales. Your consumers could
be anywhere in the world, buying via the world wide web, an environment that
crosses traditional international borders with a click.

Of course, there's also the more visible global business world: the physical
transportation of products, establishment of branches, set-ups with distribution
partners or sales reps, ex-patriot assignments, financial transactions or even the
execution of documents. No wonder there are scads of regulations in play.

Despite the fact that the *international* aspect of this business sounds—and
is—really cool, it significantly increases the complexity and risks you face. If you
see opportunity out there, you will encounter all the usual business issues, with the
added layer of at least one completely different country (with perhaps significantly
different jurisdiction) to also consider.

So it should come as no surprise that we emphatically recommend that you
educate yourself, get reliable advice, and develop a business plan before you make

any commitment to international business. By that we mean a plan for your first venture, and then separate plans for new territories as you expand.

Major considerations to address in your international business plan

Not all, but many of the factors you'll need to think through are legal matters. Some are financial, and then there's a whole rainbow of other things. Since in many ways these things are inseparable, we want to get you thinking in a broad, long-term mindset. Here are some of the major items to consider about potential international business.

Legal Systems If you must use your target country's legal system, can you even do so? Will it work? Is it cost effective and reasonably transparent? Are you able to reasonably predict the outcome? Do you have qualified legal representation there? Things will be simpler in a country with a legal system similar to yours and with established professionals (lawyers or barristers) who speak your language. In contrast, doing business in a distant country, one that speaks another language and is based on tribal systems where you are expected to pay an unknown tribute amount to the local establishment for an unknown result, will demand more patience, flexibility, caution, and long-term commitment.

Political Systems What are the target country's systems of government at all levels—national, regional and local? How would they affect your business? How stable are those political systems? What roles do corruption, bribery and organized crime play? If systems are likely to change, what is the probable effect on your business? Stable systems tend to support more business, with less risk and generally lower average returns on investment (due to higher competition), as compared to many developing or recently peaceful countries that have significantly lower stability, higher risk, but also higher potential returns. There may be good news for entrepreneurs considering the latter countries: any of the international investment treaties discussed below will have significant incentives for businesses to encourage them to invest there.

Labor Standards Many companies, small and large, have outsourced various parts of their businesses overseas: manufacturing operations to China, technical support to India or documentary support to South America. The reason? Reduced labor costs and benefits like 24/7 workdays. Consider questions like these. What are the local employment requirements? What are the wage rates and what's forecasted for them? Are these cost effective for your operations? What is the quality of the workforce population? Is there any potential for becoming involved in undesirable practices like child labor, or situations where you may attract bad business publicity for operating out of these specific countries?

Local Culture and Other Considerations Will the local culture support or threaten your business model? For example, in some cultures, copying is the highest form of praise. What impact will that have on your activity? Are there language barriers or educational barriers that would affect business? What is the local work schedule? Are there any religious, tribal or other factors that need to be considered? The examples in this category are rich and abundant, from differences in workdays, daily working hours, translated product names that have offensive meanings in local slang; plus vast cultural differences in management, hierarchy and communication methods.

Environmental Issues What are the local concerns and regulations related to the environment? If your home country's rules are tougher, then which should you follow? What is the potential for damage from a natural disaster (earthquake, monsoon) or an environmental emergency? Are there ethical dilemmas related to locally legal but admittedly harmful practices? Waste generation and disposal, sustainable development, emissions, long-term damage and potential liability related to harm done are very real issues here. Examples of these tough issues are in every day's news.

Infrastructure This is an area where it pays to see things first-hand if your target country is underdeveloped or starting its ascent. Are roads, utilities, communication systems and port or rail facilities reliable? Do other companies with experience in your target country have tales to tell about patchwork solutions, and are you willing to work that way? What future improvements are planned, and who's funding them?

Import/Export Trade Regulations Some very complex considerations get involved here, and you need to evaluate them extremely carefully. Key factors include your product, country, shipping method, prices, etc. These could be affected by tariffs, quotas, trade agreements, standards regulation, regional preferences, popular opinion, etc. Your product may not sell well vs. locally made products, or import fees or taxes may make it too expensive to compete well, or it may not meet technical standards of quality or measurement. On the other hand, you could benefit from programs that give incentives to invest in the training and deveopment of the target country's workforce, or from other sorts of consideration.

Transactions Costs and Exchange Rates Transaction costs include the freight and the extra layers needed to supervise transport of supplies and products; the risk involved in potential loss, damage or delay of shipments; variation in currency exchange rates that could affect profitability; costs to meet local regulatory and accounting requirements; local tax considerations and more.

Major Tax Considerations International tax strategy and planning is a huge, complicated deal, with many Fortune 500 companies reaping significant profits as a result. Many countries, including Ireland, Bermuda, the Cayman Islands and Luxembourg, among others, structure their tax codes to attract international business and investment. As your revenues increase along with your international presence, this can become a long-term strategic consideration.

At this point you probably are having second thoughts, at least about pulling together a sound business plan. Don't feel pressed to rush through this, and do get advice from your network and your legal and tax advisors to help fill in the blanks. Doing this will reduce the number of blanks left, highlighting the remaining ones, so you can see what you'll need to find out and weigh before you take binding decisions.

M.R.M. and S.G.

CHAPTER II

Legal Issues

Loading Up Your Legal Toolbox

The nice thing about legal issues in your international business is that you probably shouldn't do the heavy lifting: your main role should be to locate and work with qualified professional advisors!

AS AN ATTORNEY, my first and most important piece of advice for you about international business is to consult with a professional who is specifically qualified to advise you on your proposed business model and the laws affecting your situation.

The ideal advisor will be well versed in the laws and culture of your home-base and target country, know a good deal about your planned activities (selling? buying? outsourcing? partnering?) and have worked with organizations of your size. Beyond these qualifications, this ideal advisor will be well connected, or else will be able to connect you with a suitable corresponding legal advisor in your target country. You may find her or his corresponding attorney invaluable in pointing you to others—bankers, managers or other talent, real estate brokers, etc. So read on, knowing that this section is only intended as a brief survey of the concepts involved to prepare you to ask good questions and develop a broad overview of what support is needed.

A grab-bag of international business

Naturally, your focus as an entrepreneur is mainly on your core business. This section places your business in its legal context as you venture abroad. Depending on your activity, you could run into challenges like these, or something entirely different—hence the need to be informed.

1. Business ownership. In China and most other communist countries, non-citizens are not allowed to own businesses. This requires even major companies like Walmart and Coke to partner with local companies and/or the government of the communist country.

2.   Local business practices. What is considered normal business varies greatly from country to country. A standard business practice in one country may be illegal in another country. For example, the customs clearance process in many developing nations involves a series of payments to local officials that would be considered bribery in most industrialized countries.

3.   Ongoing conflicts. As you know, many groups of people are involved in ongoing conflicts with other groups of people, based on past events, or on religious or tribal differences. You must factor these situations in when doing business with these groups. For example, companies in many of the Muslim countries will not do business with you if your products have any components manufactured in Israel.

4.   Increased regulation by a foreign country. Some countries will substantially increase regulations or standards as a method of setting global policy. For example, most of the Norse countries (Sweden, Finland, Norway) enforce significantly higher environmental standards than are required by any international rules or by most other countries. To do business in these countries you must comply with their environmental standards.

5.   Maritime laws. The law of the high seas is the original international law jurisdiction. This area is rife with unique examples and interesting cases. For example, most countries distinguish between cargo transport by a tugboat (push) and a towboat (pull) in terms of contract requirements, taxation and liability. Also, the "flag" a ship flies is the jurisdiction it has registered in, and that dictates the legal system that governs the actions of the ship. Visit any port and you will see international law in action.

An ounce of prevention is worth a pound of cure...

To understand the legal issues you may face in your international business operations, you (or better, your advisor) must do quite a bit of research before you finalize your plans.

- Start with a review of the laws of your business's home country as they relate to international business dealings.

- Then review the laws and legal system of the foreign country in which you intend to do business.

- Next, review the specific laws or agreements between your country and that foreign country.

- Finally, review the international regulations or standards that may affect your business operations.

If your legal review doesn't reveal insurmountable obstacles, that's good news. If you identify problem areas, you'll need to think through the degree of risk you feel you can take on. If you see opportunities but have reasonable doubts, you may find it worthwhile to reduce the risk through insurance products. Or if you see too many potential problems, be glad you didn't run into them in day-to-day operations abroad, and perhaps consider a different target market. Just do your homework carefully.

Domestic laws affecting international business

These are the laws of your country that affect both domestic and international business. For example, if you are manufacturing a product in your home country to export for distribution and sale overseas, you will still be required to comply with your local labor and employment laws, such as overtime pay or working conditions, regardless of the laws in the foreign country in which you intend to sell your products. Even if goods or services are leaving your country, that does not release you from compliance with your local laws.

In addition to observing standard local business laws, you will need to verify whether your country places any additional legal requirements or awards special benefits on your particular industry. For example, many high technology products (nuclear energy, aerospace) may have limited international distribution due to national security concerns, while other areas such as food production (corn, coffee) or emerging and critical sectors (renewable energy, transportation) may have programs established to subsidize your business model and aid in the profitability of your business, if it is declared to be in your country's national interest.

Types of legal systems throughout the world

You probably are quite familiar with the legal system where your company is based. But you may not know much about the system in your target market, and you need to. Each foreign country and region is unique, and each has individual legal systems designed for the benefit of their citizens. Take a moment to familiarize yourself with the basic systems, their strengths and weaknesses, and then identify which system you'll be dealing with abroad.

Most legal systems fall into three main types:

- Common law
- Civil law
- Religious law

They may operate separately, or you may find or some combination of the three types. Regardless of what you discover, is important to understand the basics about the legal system of the foreign country where you are doing business.

Common law is a system of laws where the legislative branch of government sets out general principles of law and the primary interpretation and development of the specific law is done by judges through court or tribunal decisions. This system is viewed as more complex than the other systems in terms of determining the actual current law, hence the increased need for a qualified professionals. Common law systems cover about a third of the world. Originally developed by the British, it is primarily used by countries affiliated with the British Empire. The primary downside to the system is the research required to understand what the current law is; while the primary benefit of the system is its ability to grow with the times, through application of the general principles to situations that could not have been predicted when the law was originally created.

Civil law is a legal system where the government codifies very specific laws. The judicial branch reviews cases on an individual basis against the codes, but does not give any merit or weight to previous decisions. Civil law systems are generally viewed as easier to understand regarding the status of the current law. Developed in the Roman Empire, it is currently used, in some form, by approximately 150 countries, including China, Russia, Brazil, Argentina, France, Germany, Japan, Mexico and Indonesia. The primary downside is the lag between a new development or issue and its codification into law, while the primary benefit is the straightforward nature of legal understanding.

Religious law may vary with the nature of the religion it relates to. The most common religion-based legal system is Islamic law or Sharia, which is a system of laws based on the principles of the Islamic religion. The primary source for the laws are the Quranic verses and the teachings of Muhammad. For issues not covered, religious scholars and Islamic judges utilize reasoning by analogy to reach decisions. These systems are viewed as religious law, with a high level of variance between the different schools of Islamic belief. This system, or some form of it, is primarily used in the Middle East, North Africa and Muslim dominated countries. The primary downside to the system is the variance in application of the law, especially to non-Muslims, while the primary benefit of the system is the synchronization of the legal system with the belief system.

Civil and criminal law

It is critical to note that in each of these systems, there is a further distinction between the "Civil" and "Criminal" sectors of the law. The basic distinctions are:

- Who can bring the action

- Who decides the outcome

- What remedies, penalties, punishments or results can be ordered

Many events can fall into both sectors of the law. There is a great degree of variance between various countries as to how these distinctions apply.

The **civil sector** generally applies to disputes between individuals, organizations or businesses. The action is brought by a private party, usually the party that has suffered harm. The party must have stake in the outcome of the case. For example, you could not file a lawsuit for someone else on a matter that you are not involved in. The action may be brought against a single party or multiple parties. Generally the party that brings a civil action is called the Plaintiff or Petitioner, while the party on the other side is known as the Defendant or Respondent. The outcome may be decided by an individual, such as a judge or magistrate, or by groups, such as a jury, tribunal or panel. The outcome is stated in terms of liability, so the defendant will be found liable, partially liable or not liable.

The results of civil actions are most often financial, as with compensation for damages, but may also include orders to do or not do a some specific thing, e.g. you *must* sell your property or you *must not* sell a particular product. It is very important to note that incarceration is not available in most civil actions. Examples of civil matters include landlord/tenant, product liability, breach of contract or personal injury issues.

The **criminal sector** generally applies to events that have been deemed illegal or criminal by a governing body. The action is brought by the governing body, usually on behalf of the victim. The victim may not even be required to participate in the legal process. The action may be brought against a single party. Most systems will require that each party charged as an individual will have an individual case. The side bringing the action is known as the Prosecution or Government, and the party on the other side is known as the Defendant. The outcome may be decided by an individual, such as a judge or magistrate, or by a group, such as a jury, tribunal or panel. However, the procedural requirements and standards of proof are often much higher in criminal matters. The outcome is stated in terms of guilt, so the defendant is found guilty or not guilty of the crime they were charged with, or of a lesser crime. The results of a criminal matter may be financial or the use of incarceration or physical punishment. Examples of criminal matters include theft, assault, trafficking or murder.

Laws between countries

Now that you have a basic understanding of the concepts of the various legal systems that could be at play within your target country, let's look the laws *between* countries. Generally, the laws governing actions between two countries and the people of each as they interact with each other are established by agreements between the sovereign states. They are known as treaties, protocols, conventions, pacts, etc. Treaties are essentially contracts between the countries. Just like the contracts that your business enters into, they can be specific or general, two-party or multi-party, binding or non-binding, modifiable or non-modifiable etc.

These agreements may be bilateral or multilateral. Bilateral treaties are agreements between two countries and multilateral ones involve more than two countries. The treaties can be very general, with very few actual requirements of action. For example, in the *Convention on the Prevention of Marine Pollution by Dumping Wastes and Other Matter (LC '72)*, the signing counties just generally agreed that they would discourage pollution through marine dumping and provided a general guide as a reference, but did not require any specific actions or interactions from the signing countries. In contrast, the *Kyoto Protocol to the United Nations Framework Convention on Climate Change* (UNFCCC) has very specific and binding obligations for the reduction of greenhouse gases by signatory countries.

Please note that even though these agreements are between the individual countries, according to the United Nations Charter, all treaties must be registered with the United Nations (UN) to be valid and enforceable. Individual countries often also have individual processes for the adoption of a treaty into law. For example, in the United States, the executive branch negotiates the treaties, but then the legislative branch must give the final approval.

Finally, changes in the geopolitical climate can have significant effects on local business. One of the main reasons free trade agreements are so controversial is because of their effects on local business, whereby many low-end manufacturing jobs and plants are exported to the lower cost countries. Another example is punitive sanctions. Very often the sanctions are on the import, export or taxation of particular goods or services to the sanctioned country. Thus the imposition of sanctions is usually intended to disrupt business with a given country.

International laws and regulations

International laws are controlled by international intergovernmental organizations, such as the UN, the European Union (EU), World Trade Organization (WTO), International Monetary Fund (IMF) and the International Maritime Organization (IMO). Each of these organizations creates laws and regulations related to their specific purpose. Most of the intergovernmental organizations also create penalties for breaking the laws. However, the power to enforce punishments is limited by the authority conferred to the organization. All intergovernmental organizations derive their authority through the voluntary participation of the member countries.

The vast majority of these countries reserve the right to punish violations of international law, within their own country. Thus, even though there maybe international laws in place, the supposed violations may only be punished if the home country declares the actions to be a violation, then sentences and punishes the guilty party for the violation.

Common examples include certain fishing practices (e.g., drag netting) and whaling. While both have been declared illegal by international law, some countries, such as Indonesia (for illegal fishing practices), and Japan and Norway (for whaling), have specifically decided not to enforce these international laws against their citizens.

Enforcement can also be an issue between countries. Often less developed nations resist being held to same standards as industrialized countries. Typical issues include work conditions, labor laws and environmental standards. The less developed countries point out that the industrialized countries were not held to those same standards while their economies modernized, and that it is inherently unfair to enforce those standards against the currently developing nations.

Other international standards

There are also additional rules and regulations by International Nongovernmental Organizations (INGOs). These include industry-based regulations like trade federations or collectives, and also philanthropic organizations such as the International Red Cross and Amnesty International. These groups are self-regulating. Participation is often voluntary.

The final area of international law to consider in relation to your business operations are the prescribed international standards. These are often sent by INGOs, such as the International Organization for Standardization (ISO) or the International Electrotechnical Commission (IEC), for the purpose of producing technical standards available for use worldwide. The adherence to these standards is often voluntary, but compliance with these standards may also be a prerequisite for entry into major markets. By the way, ISO is something like a brand name. As the ISO website explains, "Because 'International Organization for Standardization' would have different acronyms in different languages (IOS in English, OIN in French for *Organisation Internationale de Normalisation*), our founders decided to give it the short form ISO. ISO is derived from the Greek *isos*, meaning equal. Whatever the country, whatever the language, we are always ISO."

Additional considerations

Other considerations you may want to review are the distinctions between goods and services under the various laws you will be subject to in your business transactions. Under the various systems there may be very different standards for personal vs. business liability that you need to be aware of. You may want to consider the political stability of the foreign country that you are doing business with, since a change in the political landscape can lead to substantial business loss. Finally, you may want to consider the nature of rights granted to you and your business by the foreign country, as many countries do not recognize property rights of non-citizens or do not enforce intellectual property rights.

Is it worth it?

You might be wondering now, with all of this to think about, if international business is really worth pursuing. The answer is yes, international business can be worth it. The world as we know it is shrinking, and globalization is an ongoing process. Even a basic trip to your local grocery store will demonstrate this to you: Just look at the labels to see the locations where your produce was grown and harvested or where that sauce you love so much was made.

We measure risk vs. return in international business, just like in all enterprises. The risks and the returns can vary greatly. Many major companies such as Walmart, Coke and McDonalds draw a substantial portion, if not the majority, of their revenues from their international operations. There's no reason your organization can't share in that wealth with a well-planned international expansion.

Remember, you do not have to be an expert in international law to run an international business, but you do need to know when to consult experts. Together you can assess your plan's odds of success.

M.R.M.

Treaties 101

You don't need to be a diplomat
to be involved with them.

WHAT IS A TREATY, ANYWAY? Think of it as a contract between two or more countries or international organizations. You may find related words like *protocols*, *conventions*, and *pacts* used instead. Treaties document agreements among the parties to do, or not to do, or to obligate themselves to either very specific points or very general guidelines.

The system of international laws that regulates cross-border business is collectively called International Commercial Law. If you plan on buying or selling goods internationally, you should know about the United Nations Convention on Contracts for the International Sale of Goods (CISG; sometimes called the Vienna Convention) and the World Trade Organization (WTO).

United Nations Convention on Contracts for the International Sale of Goods (CISG)

The CISG is the convention for the sale of goods that cross international borders. If you own a US business which makes birdhouses, and you buy all of your materials from Amazon.com, eBay.com or other reputable importers, you don't need to worry about this. Those merchants have already dealt with all applicable regulations for the materials they resell to you.

There is one thing to keep in mind with the CISG: not all countries abide by it. Because it's a United Nations organization, only members of the United Nations honor it. If you decide to directly import from or export to another country, make sure you research that country's regulations adequately. Generally, most countries in Africa, Asia, Europe (Eastern and Western), Latin America, and the Caribbean participate in CISG. The United Nations hosts a website fully dedicated to CISG, also known as UNCITRAL (visit uncitral.org). They provide basic facts about international trade, along with frequently asked questions. The site is currently published in six languages.

The World Trade Organization (WTO) is organized under a treaty, but it functions as more of a centralized record keeper or secretary. It supports international trade and provides a common structure for trade relations between contracting parties. The main objective of the WTO is to consider issues like tariff classifications, product nature, intended use, commercial value, price, and sustainability in order to minimize discrimination between imported and domestic products. The WTO has no actual authority to create or enforce trade agreements. All treaties are subject to change at any time by the countries that have signed them. Therefore changes in regimes, government types or controlling parties could potentially affect any trade agreements.

Here are a few more important treaties that could affect your company abroad:

- The North American Free Trade Agreement (NAFTA) creates a trading bloc between the United States, Canada and Mexico, somewhat like the European Union.

- The Kyoto Protocol is an international agreement linked to the United Nations Framework Convention on Climate Change. It sets binding international emission reduction targets.

- The Patent Law Treaty is designed to streamline, harmonize and simplify the formal requirements set by national or regional patent offices in relation to applying for and maintaining patents.

These or other treaties may have specific effects on your business model and/or profitability. You will need to do your homework and perhaps consult the appropriate professionals in relation to your business. Note: In addition to attorneys and tax advisors, there are businesses and consultants who specialize in facilitating international trade.

Protection and free trade

There is an ongoing source of conflict related to international trade agreements. The competing positions are the protection of special industries by the industrialized countries vs. support for completely free trade by the developing nations. The primary industries involved here are agriculture and new technology. The industrialized countries want to protect their domestic agriculture sector through subsidies and tariffs to ensure that their countries will have enough food in the event of a famine or war. The developing countries are pushing for free trade on agriculture because that is a sector in which a developing nation could immediately compete, based on available land and cheap labor.

These conflicts continue into new or high tech industries which the political decision makers view as a future source of income or power. Such industries, e.g., computers or solar power, are often heavily subsidized by governments to ensure they grow within that country, even if they are not profitable. The heavy subsidies make it impossible for developing nations to compete in these sectors.

International business is a very real possibility for many businesses, even tiny start-ups, given today's globalized market. There is a lot to learn and consider, but by taking the time to think about it and factor it into your business plan, you will be better prepared to identify and develop opportunities in the long run.

S.G. and M.R.M.

Tariffs and Quotas and Trade, Oh My!

*Just the basics, so you can see
if you need to dig deeper.*

TO MANY ENTREPRENEURS, even those exploring international business, tariffs and quotas are subjects they skim past in the news. And in fact, their goods may not be affected by them. But it's smart to be informed, and you may in fact be affected. So here's your starter course.

What is a tariff?
It's a tax or a fee placed on the import or export of goods. Today, tariffs are heavily debated in various economic theories, with the arguments focusing, as ever, on protectionism vs. free trade. Tariffs have a strong connection with various political movements and have been very controversial throughout history. Well-known examples of tariffs include the British trade restrictions which led to the Boston Tea Party and sparked the American Revolution in the 18th Century, and the US's Smoot-Hawely Tariff Act, which significantly increased tariffs just as the Great Depression of the 1930s was beginning. This tariff sparked immediate retaliatory tariffs by most of the country's trading partners and is widely believed to have significantly contributed to the severity and length of the Depression.

Since World War II, the general view of free trade has been more positive and tariffs have been steadily reduced, playing a smaller role in international business and fiscal policy. However, there are still some significant tariffs in place on items like paper clips, canned tuna, sneakers, peanuts, tires and steel.

Countries use tariffs to protect a particular industry and to raise revenue. The government may decide to protect a specific industry because it is a newly established or developing industry (in the US, think of renewable energy technologies); it is an inefficient but critical industry (steel, agriculture); or because foreign companies are "dumping" in the industry, meaning that the foreign companies are flooding the market with below-market-value priced products with the intention of monopolizing the industry. The added cost to an import will make it easier for domestic products to compete and the added cost to an export will make it more likely that the good is not exported to that location.

Tariffs can be charged as a percentage of value or as a flat fee based on quantity. The revenues from the tariff go directly to the government. At one time this was the largest source of income for the US federal government.

What is a quota?

Quotas are another economic government control measure used primarily to protect domestic producers and industries. Quotas are set by the government and specify an exact quantity of a particular good that may be exported or imported. They are a strongly protectionist control measure and are viewed as potentially harmful to a free-market economy, as they do not allow for any competition from foreign products and result in higher prices to consumers. Quotas are also called "non-tariff trade barriers". The history of trade quotas is very similar to that of tariffs—a popular, but controversial fiscal tool whose use has declined significantly after World War II.

There are a number of key industries in the US that still have substantially limiting and controversial quotas in place. Those industries include sugar, tobacco, cotton, beef, anchovies, olives, Mandarin oranges and brooms. Other countries protect other industries, so check on their positions.

Fortunately, unless you are in a specifically regulated industry, the current tariffs and quotas should have very little effect on your business planning. If you are in one of those particular industries, then you will need to forecast any changes in trade policy in order to position your business for success.

M.R.M.

Immigration Issues

*This area is fairly complex, so consider getting
an attorney's input if issues arise.*

EACH COUNTRY HAS ITS OWN RULES, regulations and laws that cover immigration and related issues. These regulations will most often be at the national and international level and enforced by national-level agencies. Sometimes there are regional regulations as well.

While each jurisdiction is unique, there are some broad categories of immigration issues that especially impact businesses: illegal immigrants, asylum seekers or refugees, guest workers, and residents and tourists.

In most large countries there is a significant **illegal immigrant** population. Illegal immigrants are people who have entered the local region in violation of the controlling immigration laws of either the local region or their region of origin. Depending on the jurisdiction, illegal immigration may or may not actually constitute a crime. Each jurisdiction has unique standards of enforcement.

Illegal immigrants may be able to switch to a legal immigration status. Employing or doing business with illegal immigrants should be considered as a business decision after evaluating the penalties and benefits under your local laws and the market conditions. There is no universal answer.

Asylum seekers or refugees are people seeking refuge in the local region, outside of their home region or country, because of persecution, fear, war or other social upheaval. They may hope to stay short term, long term or permanently. There are international treaties and United Nations Conventions related to the definition and treatment of refugees. Generally speaking, upon arrival in the local region, the refugee must apply for asylum based on the above reasons. If the application is approved, she will be granted legal status in the local region, based on her circumstances.

Guest programs include guest workers and students. Some countries rely very heavily on guest worker programs to supplement their workforces. Guest worker programs are often controversial, as standards regarding the rights of guest workers and students while in the local region are not evenly enforced. International students and study abroad programs are also very common in our globalized world.

Guest worker status is a legal immigration designation given to foreign workers who temporarily work and live in the local region. Both the qualifications and the difficulty in acquiring this status change often and by jurisdiction. Usually guest-worker status is given to high-skill positions or to areas with an extreme shortage of available labor.

Student programs are similar in that they allow a legal immigration status for a certain period while the student participates in continuing education. If a student remains beyond the term specified, his status could change to being an illegal immigrant.

Almost all countries have immigration provisions dealing with **residents and tourists**. Residents are non-citizens who have been granted permission to live in the local region indefinitely. Individual jurisdictions may have ongoing requirements to seek citizenship or to contribute to the economy in some way. In countries already associated as trading partners, such as the European Union, the requirements are significantly easier.

Tourists are major economic driver and source of revenues for certain regions. Each jurisdiction will have individual requirements for documentation, length of stay, removal of goods and more. Generally speaking, tourism is encouraged but regulated.

M.R.M.

Immigration: Opportunities and Challenges

Talent, energy—and potential customers—
are moving around as never before.

WHAT IS IMMIGRATION? It's people moving into and settling in a non-native country or region. That movement can be international, regional or even local. Nowadays, practically all businesses have some experience with immigration and its effects on the workplace, whether it be in a business's home base or its operations in target markets abroad.

All over the world, immigration is an extremely complex, often controversial topic. It may be welcomed or opposed by the local population and represent dreams-come-true or nightmares for the immigrant. Immigration is a source of population growth and cultural change, but also of concern and conflict.

Factors that encourage immigration include open or porous borders, better opportunities, cheap land, rumors of instant wealth, higher pay, family reunification, better social welfare, better schools, political freedoms or religious callings. In countries generally considered to be economically open, immigrants often make up an extremely large percentage of the small-business community, perhaps because it may be easier to start a little business than to find work as an employee, or because entrepreneurial opportunity is what attracted the immigrant in the first place.

As globalization and international business shrink our planet every day, the ease with which people may move throughout the world in search of better opportunities is rising. This has caused immigration and closely related issues to be on the forefront of the political debates in most countries or regions. The exact issues vary greatly, depending on the location, but as a businessperson you should be aware of all of the political trends or pressures in all of the areas that your business operates. These political movements could include separatist movements, civil unrest, cultural conflicts, and restrictive or open immigration policies.

Looking for opportunities

People from elsewhere are very likely settling in your area now. They may come as political refugees, as workers seeking better opportunities, as invited members of a thriving ethnic community, as migrant workers, as investors, etc. They may prefer to preserve their own culture or choose to assimilate and adopt the local culture.

As immigrants interact with your business, their legal status could present both opportunities and legal issues for you, due to employment, taxation or other regulations. Seasonal immigration patterns could have significant practical effects on business as well.

Local patterns could include the development and growth of an immigrant community with a strong cultural identification. This could create or eliminate a market or source of labor and talent for your business's services or products. You need to know the answers to questions like these:

- Are these communities growing or shrinking?

- Are they integrating with surrounding and local cultures?

- Do they bring particular assets or interests you can tap for your business's growth?

- Are you part of this community? Can you develop connections, if not?

- Are there steps your business could take to capture this market for your goods or services, or tap its human resources for your workplace?

- Are there language differences or barriers you need to be aware of?

- Are there charitable or humanitarian things your business can do with or for the immigrants?

Often, simple small steps can make all the difference. For example, do you have your menu or website translated into the immigrants' language? (And by the way, do you take non-native speakers' needs into account in your company's documents, from internal policy manuals to signage in your shops for non-native speaking tourists, etc.?) Do you observe cultural distinctions or holidays that your immigrant colleagues observe? Finally, given the share of your target market that this particular community makes up, are there any competitors better poised to capture the market?

Seasonal migrations and "gold rushes"

Seasonal migrations can also affect businesses on many levels. These migratory patterns often can have significant ramifications for employees, consumers and others. Migratory workers usually follow peak labor needs in agriculture, fisheries, and in other sectors with defined planting, processing or harvest seasons. As many farmers have learned the hard way, a significant event affecting one crop can have a major impact on the migration patterns of workers, and consequently the farmers' costs and ability to effectively bring their crop to market.

From time to time around the world, a resource is discovered or a region or city starts a huge construction project, and these things attract workers as well. Your business might be on the fringe of all the frantic activity. It might gain or lose from the surge.

Emigration

Think of emigration as immigration, but viewed from the immigrant's original home base, with a focus on the loss of those who go away. Emigrants are those who leave a homeland or region. Their departures affect many regions and countries throughout the world.

Common examples include the brain drain, where educated and professional individuals study and then stay abroad, or go abroad after studies and create talent and knowledge shortages back home. Or the mass emigrations we've witnessed, away from rural and agricultural areas to urban economies worldwide, leaving not only no workers, but also no heirs for the family farms. These trends can cause costs of products to rise and fall, and ditto for business opportunities. Factors that generally push people to leave an area include natural disasters (drought, monsoon, volcanic eruption), high unemployment, lack of rights, land shortages, resource depletion, oppressive conditions or persecution, warfare, famine or expulsion.

What does this mean for my business?

Good question. Immigration patterns may have deep, far-reaching effects on your business. They could come in the form of economic, social, political, health, crime, environmental, educational or local attitude effects.

Economic effects are often the most apparent in the business context. Does this immigrant population provide a new market or workers for your business? Will it increase or decrease your costs? What does it mean for your revenues and profits?

Social effects are influenced by the prevailing social norms of both the local population and the immigrant population. Sometimes there is resistance and even opposition to immigration by local populations; but other times, strong preferences for immigrants dominate. Resistance can take the form of general opposition, racism or xenophobia. Preferences range from hiring British-accented telephone receptionists in locations outside the United Kingdom where their accent lends a feeling of "class" to the operation, to hiring mine workers willing to do hard labor for low wages.

Political effects are evident in your daily news. All the issues we touch on in this section are capable of generating tremendous political change, policy review, and heated discussion, if not street warfare. Virtually every business today is affected by immigration in some way.

Health concerns of immigration include the actual health of a population, the customs of a particular group and their impact on immigrants' health, their access to local health care and their actual or potential exposure to disease. Health issues directly correlate to immigrants' ability to look for immediate employment or their need for certain services. What access to health care services does your new immigrant worker have? Could that influence his ability to recover from illness and return to work?

Crime and corruption may occur, and affect your business, when immigration is prevalent. When people are displaced, they can become easy prey for criminals or exploiters. Immigrants might target other immigrants or local people, and local people might target immigrants. On the other hand, some immigrant communities have a much lower incidence of crime than the general population. This could be due to cultural norms or the close-knit nature of the group.

Also you should consider the **cultural norms of business** held by different groups. In some cultures it is considered rude to negotiate or to talk business without first discussing social matters like children and families. Others expect spirited give and take on pricing, and paying an initial asking price is never an option. Bribes or tips for good service are required in some cultures and never given in others. These norms tend to migrate along with people, so as you interact in business with immigrant counterparts, be aware of the norms that are in play.

The environmental concerns of immigration include the exploitation of all available resources for use vs. conservation, as well as overloads on public services when immigrant groups arrive *en masse* in an area. And people of different origins may have different standards regarding environmentally sound practices. Newcomers used to keeping and slaughtering chickens in the back yard may conflict with local ordinances. These issues often have long-term effects on the local environment and/or public opinion towards particular populations.

Educational considerations include the current language skills and education level of the immigrant population (and therefore your consumers or employees), their access to further education, and finally the long-term educational opportunities for subsequent generations. The current level is the most immediate concern for your business. If immigrants are your consumers, then you need to consider their language skills and education level when planning where and how you advertise, what you say on your packaging, etc. If you tap the group for workers, you need to consider language and education levels and adjust them in your hiring, training, employment and managing practices.

Ongoing education is another factor you should consider in developing immigrant workers' productivity and value. Supporting education at home is important too. Generally speaking, if your company's practices value education, and for example offer flex-time scheduling to allow workers to attend school or be involved in their children's school activities, everybody benefits. Cultures that value childhood education tend to be more stable.

Building a plan

The local attitudes towards immigration and immigrant groups should be factored into your business planning. In our globalized world, some form of this issue is near the top of the political debate in most regions. Whether it is related to the open or restrictive nature of the general policy, the legal status of protectionist measures of certain industries, or other issues, it is a heated debate. Your decision as a business owner to interact with immigrants could have short- and long-term effects on your business operations and should be reviewed carefully and periodically.

The economic or other conditions of the home country should also be considered in planning in relation to immigrant populations. For instance, the resolution of a home country conflict could lead to a mass movement back to the home region and a loss of employees or consumers for your business. Or a shift in the currency exchange rate back home could be a significant factor in determining what wage an immigrant may need to earn as your employee.

Finally, it's important to remember that many immigrants have specific goals that motivate them: to get an education and move back home, to earn money and send it home, to save enough money to move the family to their location or to attain local citizenship. These goals should also be considered in your business planning. You can't predict the future, but you can consider it in advance.

M.R.M.

CHAPTER III

Financials

Finding Money Abroad

Think global, bank local?

AMONG THE MANY TOP-PRIORITY ISSUES you face as you consider taking your business into a market abroad is how to handle your finances there. Most entrepreneurs ultimately decide it is best, or even necessary, to work with a bank in the target market and perhaps secure some form(s) of capital resources locally. They find that this allows the segment of their business that is operating in the target market to work more smoothly and move more quickly toward a state of sustainability, rather than being completely bound to the laws, structures and relationships of the home country. Their local banking needs can be handled in real time by people who will come to know your business, and that can give the local company flexibility and responsiveness which is important for long-term success.

Financial support and your plans

The physical location where you plan to start or expand and the type of industry in which your business operates will greatly influence the array of opportunities that may exist for government subsidies, private investors, institutional investors and your ability to borrow and have access to credit. If you are at the very start of your research into where to expand internationally, try to discover what countries or regions and cities within them might be especially welcoming and encouraging to your type of operation. It might not have occurred to you that Country X could be a good prospect, but if you put Country X through all the other evaluations you are giving to countries that first come to mind, you might find some interesting opportunities.

The nature of banks in your target market

Let's say you have firmly decided on your target country. In my opinion, the first step in pursuing international capital resources is to identify the structure and the stability of conventional banking in that country. This is important because you will most likely have accounts with them, and some of your business's operating budget will be placed into accounts with them, so it would be a great first step just to check everything out. Some banks are more business-friendly than others. Also, try to assess the relative safety a candidate bank can offer you. You probably wouldn't want to have your money in banks in a war zone.

Once you've determined that using a local bank and its services makes sense as part of your expansion, ask if there are any international banks in the area that have offices and additional locations anywhere near your headquarters. When Scott and I worked with a trading company in China, it was helpful that the bank that we worked with had branches in China, Hong Kong and also in Chicago (close to our home base). This made it extremely easy to move capital around and electronically manage certain expenses of our projects remotely. Most important, we were in control of the cash flow and we could manage our own budgets without having to hire, train and trust someone on the other end. Now, that being said, as time went on we did eventually work with a few human capital resources in China and in Hong Kong that we allowed limited access to money and certain accounts in an effort to help the business run smoothly and more efficiently.

One practical tip: consider opening two accounts in your target market bank. Use one to wire in operating cash, but authorize the person who pays local expenses like salaries only to draw from a second account. Weekly (or at whatever frequency works), your local manager can submit a list of expenses for you to approve for payment. You transfer that amount (or more) to the account that your manager can access, and ensure the local business can run smoothly without risking unapproved expenditures.

Private investors and immigration incentive plans

Another interesting strategy for finding funding abroad is to identify private investors who may have an interest in your business or industry, or who simply want to benefit from one of the many immigration programs that support and incentivize foreign investors to participate in business and the economic growth of a country.

For example, the United States offers a program through the US Citizenship and Immigration Services called "Green Card Through Investment". It allows entrepreneurs, their spouses and any unmarried children under 21 years of age, who invest in a commercial enterprise in the United States that plans to either create or preserve ten full-time jobs for qualified United States workers, to apply for a green card (which permits permanent residence in the US). The required investment amounts range from $500,000 to over $1,000,000, depending on the nature of the investment.

Economic growth incentives

Certain countries offer incentives that are unrelated to immigration. They simply want to stimulate economic activity and growth. Therefore you and your business may be eligible for grants, loans or other forms of aid that will help you seamlessly move your operation, start a business abroad or expand into new markets. Often this type of help can come in other ways that reach far beyond money, such as fast-track approvals, certifications and licensing requirements. This help can be very important, because depending on your business, it can be the regulatory side, not the capital side of the initiative, that can ruin an opportunity.

Caution, creative searching and win-win deals

Either way, when searching for money abroad, the most important things to remember are to really vet the financial resources you plan to use, and to feel confident about their stability within the local economy. Also, make sure that you are effectively investigating all of the resources that may be available to you for expanding into certain countries and market areas. Most importantly, try to find local private investors who would find it advantageous to invest or partner with you and your organization in some way. Mutually beneficial, win-win business deals tend to work out the best for all parties involved, and these types of businesses tend to grow more smoothly and much faster than those that attempt to do everything themselves.

M.O.

Moving Money Across Borders

Managing money globally can be tricky for individuals;
managing a business's money internationally can be
even trickier... and more expensive.

HERE'S A QUESTION for you. How should you move your business's money across national borders for a transaction?

Say, for instance, you own a T-shirt screen printing shop in Seattle, Washington in the US, and you've decided to start purchasing your blank T-shirts in bulk from China. At high volume, the Chinese just couldn't be beat for blank T-shirt pricing. Once you get your truckloads of T-shirts, you'll print catchy stuff on them, and sell them all over town. You and your Chinese source have already done all the preliminary talks and signed a contract, and as soon as they get the money for the first shipment, they will begin production on your shirts.

The easiest way to get your money to China would be to stuff the cash in a big box and ship it, right? No. Don't be surprised when your national immigration and customs officials show up at your door and take you to prison.

Look, hopefully you've gathered by now that going global with your business is exciting and rewarding, but also far from easy. If something seems too good (or easy) to be true, it probably is. Everything has a cost, and if you're not paying somebody something, you might want to ask yourself why. There's a more than decent chance that as long as you take special care not to break any national or international laws while you venture across borders with your business, you and your business will be just fine... but probably paying more than you need to. And that's what this section is about: NOT paying more than you need to in order to move your business's money across borders.

Taxes and service fees

As you have no doubt discovered, global money management depends, by and large, on your business's country of origin, your target market, the type of business you're in, the number of local nationals you plan to employ, etc., etc., etc. Once you start doing business abroad, there are two terms you will quickly become tired of seeing on your invoices and other paperwork: *service fee* and *tax*.

Tax breaks vary with all different possible business scenarios. When first looking for a foreign country with which to do business, don't just pay attention to the vendor that will give you the lowest price on good or services. Pay close attention to the country in which that business is located, and even the city or province, because local taxes and fees apply in certain areas, too. Beyond costs, payment terms can vary among areas, so while it's smart to shop around for the best value of products, it's also smart to research and examine for consideration the local government terms that could also affect your bottom-line profits.

Converting currencies

Before you pay your first international tax, you will likely see bank or credit card service fees from currency exchanges. Money is money, right? Yes, but try to pay for your double-tall-nonfat-light whip-no water-coffee delicacy at Starbucks in the US with some Chinese bank notes you found in your pocket from your last trip. The barista will look at you like you have two heads, because most United States businesses don't take foreign currencies. And there's a fair reason why.

Whoever ends up with the Chinese notes will eventually have to exchange them for dollars. And guess what: People who exchange money don't do it for free. As with most transactions, it's never a flat *fee*; it's a flat *rate*. So if you exchange US$5.00 for Chinese renminbi, the transaction fee might only be 5 cents (assuming the exchange rate is 1%... although between 1 per cent and 3 per cent is normal).

But if you just bought 100,000 blank T-shirts for US$2.00 each, that is a US$200,000 invoice and about $2,000 in exchange fees that someone is going to have to pay. Also, because people really like taking your money, you'll typically pay an exchange rate *adjustment* fee AND an exchange rate *transaction* fee.

It's uncommon for the buyer of goods to be asked to pay for the exchange fees, but it's not impossible, especially if the seller knows you are new to international business. The best way to ensure you're not stuck with this is to ensure this topic is addressed during your up-front negotiations. You may even find foreign companies who quote, sell and receive payments in the US dollar entirely, in order to avoid exchange fees.

Bi-lateral netting

Suppose your company is big enough to have its own subsidiaries in other countries as part of an internal supply chain (e.g., you own a T-shirt factory in China and a T-shirt screen printer and store in Indonesia). You want the subsidiaries to pay each other across borders, and you, the parent company, keep all the bottom-line profits at the end of the day. You may benefit from something called bi-lateral netting.

Bi-lateral netting happens when two subsidiaries of the same company located in two different countries trade goods. For the sake of this scenario, say that the Chinese, who make blank T-shirts, would like buy some of the shirts back from the Indonesian screen printer to resell in China after the catchy stuff gets printed on them.

- So China produces and sells blank T-shirts to your Indonesian subsidiary for US$200,000.

- Indonesia prints catchy stuff on them and sends a portion of the printed shirts back to China so China can sell the printed shirts, charging the Chinese US$100,000 for them.

- A lot of money just exchanged hands between China and Indonesia, namely a total of US$300,000. And both transactions incurred exchange fees and taxes. Seems silly (and a little unfair), right? That brings us back to bi-lateral netting.

Bi-lateral netting is a concept whereby two subsidiaries sign documentation declaring they will only actually pay the *net* of the tangible related transactions. Since Indonesia only netted US$100,000 from China, that is all the money that actually exchanges hands. And presto! The exchange fee drops by two-thirds.

There are many more ways you can save on the transaction costs of moving money across borders. While your banker stands to gain from them, she ought to also be able to advise you about secure, legal ways to minimize the cost of money in your particular case. The better informed your banker is about your business, the more helpful she can be to you. And if you prosper, so will her bank. So it pays to learn as much as you can and think creatively with your bankers, both at home and in your target market, to make money moves as efficient and low-cost as possible.

S.G.

Currency Fluctuations and Cures

*A mix of smart practices and patience is called for in
the currency game. A lot is out of your control.*

IN INTERNATIONAL BUSINESS, one of the most critical elements that you
need to manage is the home currency you use and its fluctuations relative to other
currencies in which you transact business. If your business is founded in the United Kingdom, your home currency will be British Pounds (GBP), but as soon as
you do any business with Euro countries, you'll be involved in currency exchange
issues.

When I travel to other countries, I'm not that concerned about the exchange
rates for food and lodging, etc. (except to feel I'm either getting gypped or getting
terrific bargains, compared to my US dollar base!) Yes, maybe I should check historical trends or look into IMF activities that could be affecting rates, but I don't,
because on a personal level I just don't convert or spend enough to justify the
amount of time necessary to maximize any efforts at getting a favorable exchange
rate. And if you use credit cards, the rates (and sometimes, "foreign currency
fees") are set by the credit card company, so it's out of your hands anyway.

However, it's not a stupid idea to manage your travel budget with rates in
mind, if you're so inclined and you travel a lot. I know plenty of people who plan
ahead for international travel, and they tend to make money by doing so. One of
my very good friends who travels to the UK often has done a wonderful job of
tracking the relationship between the US dollar (USD) and the GBP. So he regularly buys GBP when the conversion is most favorable, and conversely, he waits
to convert his GBP back to USD until the rate becomes favorable again. Planning
ahead allows him to maximize the value of both currencies throughout the year
for his own benefit.

There have even been a few times when he actually made quite a lot of
money. Some years ago he bought GBPs when the buy price for one British

Pound was around US$1.50. He later sold his unspent GBPs when the buy price was US$2.01! The guy cleverly made an almost 25 per cent return on his money.

Now just imagine what would have happened if a business had done the necessary research, analysis and forecasting to predict that these types of fluctuations could happen. Wait! They do. Believe it or not, some international businesses have entire investment teams that focus on currency markets, future values and relationships based on all sorts of inputs. However, let's leave the details for another book.

The rate game

The point is that successfully forecasting currencies can make or break an international deal. That's especially true in situations such as contract manufacturing, which is something that Scott and I used to do a lot in Southeast Asia, years ago. To make this example short and sweet, imagine this scenario.

- On Day One of a project you get initial production quotes from a factory. You work out an acceptable price with your vendor and name the currency and payment terms. Then, you send your own tooling and other specialty materials to the manufacturer. By now we are 60 days into the project.

- Next, the actual production of your goods starts. It takes four to six weeks, maybe even longer. So now we are roughly four months into the project. The goods are finally ready to ship.

- At this point you have to arrange the shipping and logistics through to the end user, warehouse or customer. The shipping from Southeast Asia to North America can take five to seven weeks on the water.

- Then, your goods have to clear customs, which can go smoothly, in a matter of a few days, or you can be randomly selected for a search, which can hold up a container for weeks.

- Once you clear customs you will most likely have to hire a dedicated transport firm to move the container of goods from the port to a warehouse to further break down the shipment into pallets, etc. This usually takes about three or four days.

As you can see, this process can take easily take four to six months. And a lot can change in the relationship between your home currency and the vendor's currency over the course of half a year!

Most projects like this are quoted Free on Board (FOB) at the factory, meaning the payment terms clock starts ticking on the day they leave the factory (i.e., you must pay 30 days later, if you get 30-day payment terms). That's why you should try to arrange terms that extend beyond your final receipt of goods. At least then your money isn't tied up while ships sail, customs officers peer and prod, and truckers haul.

Currency options

As we've just seen, it is important to make sure your transactions are backed by contract language that not only sets pricing, but also locks in the currency conversion rate. If your vendor can't agree to that, you can buy *currency options* to protect yourself against fluctuation. Basically, they are a contract (often with your bank) that gives you the right to buy or sell a certain amount of a specific currency, at a certain rate, within a defined period of time. But you don't have to exercise your option if the currency fluctuates in your favor. If that happens, simply don't use your option and benefit from the positive change in value. If the currency in question shifts the other way, then at least you are protected. Note that there are lots of variations on the currency option theme, so it's a good idea to make sure you are using the best form for your purposes and ask lots of questions before you sign up.

Currency options cost money, of course, so sometimes, you may be better off working out some creative payment terms with your vendor (making him your banker). Compare the costs and risks and do your best. In international business, these currency fluctuations are part of the game.

M.O.

Making Sure You Get Paid, Protecting What's Yours

Don't get so excited when you make a sale or place an order at a great price that you forget to look after your business's interests.

YES, BELIEVE IT OR NOT, getting paid is a common problem in international business, especially between two businesses located in different countries which do not jointly recognize a single, overarching regulatory body (something you can avoid within the European Union, for example). And yet there are opportunities to be had that can make you want to take the risk. The same goes for finding a terrific price offered by a new vendor. You can pay for mistakes in multiples of the price savings you thought you would gain.

Risky business?

Suppose you want to start doing business in an emerging market. You may soon discover that there are no uniform or standardized processes in that country, and there's a complete lack of government infrastructure and financial regulation. If you still want to pursue the opportunity, you would be wise to protect your company's interest via receiving payment in advance, or using third party banking and escrow services.

However, it's not always so difficult. Most deals between businesses that cross countries' boundaries are either regulated by an organization such as the EU, trade treaties such as the North American Free Trade Agreement (NAFTA) or other governmental structures that allow for cooperative enforcement of fair trade practices, contract law, business law, etc. These types of helpful organizations tend to be available with developed countries and also those that are focused on capitalism and economic growth.

Just remember, not unlike any other types of investments, the most secure opportunities with the least risk will often yield the least reward. As the cliché goes, and as every entrepreneur learns one way or another, risk and reward are directly related.

Insuring invoices and factoring

Two kinds of for-profit financial services can help you ensure you get money due you. First, you can insure your invoices to qualified customers (whose stability is measured by the service offering this protection after looking at their financial records). That way you know that you'll receive at least a decent percentage of any defaulted payment. Or you can set up a factoring agreement, where the factoring company collects your payments due and retains a commission for chasing the money down. These services obviously reduce your bottom line, but it may be a question of getting something or nothing in extreme cases. And by the way, these services may be helpful to your cash flow even if you only do domestic business. In remote or developing countries, you may not be able to find this kind of coverage.

It's not only about getting paid

Getting paid—or not—is highly visible. But let's not forget that your other assets, like materials, equipment and such, are like cash on your balance sheet. It's important to look after them in your international business ventures as well.

One time we started working with a factory in another country that was recommended to us by a contact. She reported they had reliably delivered for years. So we naïvely went into the deal with a little bit more trust than we probably should have had. Don't get me wrong: We still used our boilerplate agreements and went through all of our usual steps. But we never really investigated how well this factory was doing financially. (Often vendors won't give you a peek into their books, but you can always get special types of insurance coverage and make other arrangements that either guarantee an outcome or at least mitigate a lot of the risk.)

So Scott and I invested quite a bit of money in raw materials and tooling to get ready for a large-scale production run. What we didn't know was that the factory was barely staying open. We trustingly purchased raw materials on a pass-through deal that put them into the factory's inventory. The company could now list our tooling set-up as if it were there own. They promptly shut down operations for good and went into liquidation—with our stuff on their factory floor, halfway around the world.

As you can imagine, when local creditors began the process of salvaging what they could from the vendor's facilities and warehouses, our investment was… let's say it was lost forever. We tried to contact various people and governmental agencies that we believed would be in control of certain aspects of the liquidation. However, that proved to be an exercise in futility. In the end, we just had to cut our losses and move on.

The moral of the story is simple: You need to make sure that you have a way of accounting for and protecting your assets. Whether they are cash, inventory, raw materials, finished goods, etc., it doesn't matter. You need to be sure that you have a clear and concise way of recovering what is yours or what is owed to you.

If you are providing materials or selling goods (and this tip goes for domestic as well as sales abroad), it's smart to have a clause printed in your invoice's terms of payment that says the goods in question remain your property until they have been fully paid for. It won't always protect you in dire situations, but it is important documentation about who owns what in case of your customer's or vendor's bankruptcy or liquidation.

Other resources

Another great way to ensure that you will get paid as agreed and on time is to work closely with local resources such as banks and law firms. Also consider trading companies that specialize in connecting international business relationships for different reasons, usually for a percentage fee of the total revenue of the business being done. I have often used resources like these over the years, not only because it eliminates or at least mitigates a lot of the risk, but also it takes a ton of work and worry off of my shoulders, allowing me to focus on other parts of my operation.

If you don't go that route, it's very easy to get bogged down by all of the minutiae and petty details that by the end of a day, week and even month leave you asking yourself what you actually got done, and where all the time went. It's just like working with a resource at home, whether it's a tax preparer or bookkeeper who charges a percent or two, or a realtor who charges five or six per cent to handle everything on your behalf and to ensure the highest and best outcome on property deals. I'm a big fan of people that have a fiduciary responsibility to either my business or me.

It's not all grim news

In short, there are many ways to get paid and protect your assets. You may have to have your customers pre-pay (and if you're just starting up your business, or starting out with a new vendor, you'll know that can apply to you as well, until you establish a track record). Other times you may request that money be put into an escrow account or be used to purchase bonds that can be held as collateral on a deal until everything is complete and payment is due. Some complex deals require working with trading companies or other professional entities that have the ability to enforce contracts and agreements within a country, due to their business structures and their understanding of local regulations and processes. In any case, there is always more than one way to skin a financial cat. You just need to evaluate your situation and make choices that work for you and your organization.

M.O.

Subsidies, Incentives and Other Start-Up Support

It's like a birthday present for your business—foreign governments give you things just for being there!

I LOVE FINDING MONEY. Any amount is fine with me. I love it when I forget that I left money in my winter coat pockets and find it a year later when the weather gets cold again. I think one of the worst pranks is when people put dog poop on a dollar and leave it on the sidewalk (poop-down), and then go hide in the bushes with a video camera and film people picking up the poop-dollar and getting excited, and then grossed-out and angry. Finding money is so much more enjoyable than earning money. Why? Because you don't expect it; you haven't worked for it; you just stumble onto it because through some mystic happenstance, the universe made it available to you.

Many national and regional governments fund incentives and subsidies for businesses, specifically to entice them to bring their business operations to their country. These incentives and subsidies can come in the form of cash grants, interest-free or low-interest loans, tax or insurance breaks, depreciation write-offs, rent or real estate rebates, and many other forms of economic intervention. With all of these, I guess you're not technically finding money, but when you're taking your business across borders, tax breaks or rent rebates you hadn't counted on in your initial business planning can be just as good!

These governments extend subsidies because your business in their country is good for them. While part of the revenue you make may go back to your home country in the form of profit and corporate taxes, that doesn't mean the country in which you're operating doesn't get a healthy slice of pie, too. Among subsidy-offering countries, you can generally estimate how much your company's operations in another country benefits them, based on how robust the subsidies and incentives will be to you. Your benefit will generally reflect how much your company's operations in the area will improve their citizens' quality of life. Will you employ local people in your office or factory? Will you have to build out infrastructure that will benefit the area, beyond your company's operations, such as a railroad, water dam, irrigation or road system, sewage plant, refinery, etc.? Or will your company's operations improve tourism?

Before the Walt Disney Company began development of Walt Disney World and the corresponding infrastructure in Orlando, Florida in the United States, Orlando wasn't much more than a few orange groves in the middle of nowhere. Walt Disney World brought a major highway, and enough infrastructure to create a new city of its own. In the years since, Orlando has grown into one of the prime tourist destinations in the world. It's safe to say that it all occurred because a big company moved to town. Tourists came because Walt Disney World was there, and more businesses came to serve those people. The economic expansion of Central Florida hasn't stopped since. As an area grows, more businesses, entrepreneurs, and employees move to the area, becoming citizens, and citizens pay taxes, which improves the local government. You can see how a business isn't just a business in the eyes of a local government; it can be a springboard to civil and economic expansion far beyond the actual operations of the business. This is why governments offer incentives to companies who will enhance the local way of life through jobs and developed infrastructure.

The movie industry often selects locations for filming movies or television shows based on incentives or subsidies offered by national or local governments. These typically come in the form of tax breaks. The reason is because when a movie company comes into town, it doesn't just bring the director, a couple actors, and a camera operator. The movie company rolls into town with hundreds, or sometimes thousands, of actors and crew.

So why would a local government offer tax breaks to a movie company that rolls into town with all their own people and stuff? There are a few reasons. First, because those hundreds of movie people spend money. They stay in local hotels, eat in local restaurants, get their cars serviced in local mechanic shops, shop in local stores, etc. Furthermore, a movie company often employs local people and companies for trade labor, catering, extra casting, etc. While film production doesn't last forever, it does typically last for a couple of months, and even that is important in the local economy.

Also, the movie industry is very chatty, and one film in a given locale may lead to another—it isn't based on just one film or television show. There are always new projects, so there's always the chance a new film production team will come to town. The National Film Board of Canada has a long list of success stories, and its support for upcoming artists is part of their core activity. Business writers are commenting on the Wimbledonization of London's business scene, meaning the attitude that it doesn't matter to the Brits who's running (or owning) what company, as long as it's good for the UK.

The movie industry is just one example of how local incentives for businesses can enhance, or even drive, a local economy, beyond the scope of the business itself. When you think about it, it really all boils down to the most basic economic principle: supply and demand. The more a local area can benefit from whatever your business could bring to it (supply), the greater their incentive for you will be (demand). It varies from area to area and from business to business.

Where do you search? First, don't overlook your home country's resources. You may find there's a local embassy or consulate with people dedicated to helping you do business in your target country. Also, almost every country, state, province, county, city, etc. has a Department of Economic Development or Ministry of State. This is typically also the location/resource for conducting official business filings with the government. If you plan on doing business abroad, that country's State Department will have most, if not all, of the information you need to know about regulations, procedures, incentives and subsidies, etc. If the department also has a website (most do), they will likely have a means to make applications for subsidies online, or at least have all the documentation you need to download, fill out and mail in.

Really, the hunt for subsidies and other incentives can be a lot of fun—just like finding that crumpled banknote in your winter coat pocket.

S.G.

Bribes and Black Money

*This is one of the more unfortunate sides of doing
business internationally. Here's a rundown of
what you can expect, and how to avoid it.*

I'M NOT YOUR MOTHER. I hope you are not surprised by this revelation. Despite this fact, I'm going to give you some advice in this section, based purely on what I've seen in the real world. When it comes to doing business internationally, bribery is out there and it can put you in prison. Black money is also out there, and can also put you in prison.

Black money, for those who are unfamiliar, is money (typically cash) that is untraced and unaccounted for by a government for taxation purposes. Black money can range from a waiter's tips not being declared as taxable income to sacks of money smuggled across borders in trucks for deposit in a foreign bank. Both kinds of transactions happen every day. You'd be surprised by what gets people hemmed up behind bars these days.

As I said, I'm not your mother, but I also don't want to see you get into trouble with these real temptations beyond your borders either. Here's another real piece of information: bribery is a slippery slope, and you never know when an off-the-books transaction will show up again in your future.

Bribery is considered a much bigger offense in some places than in other parts of the world. The United States, Canada, Australia and Western Europe see bribery as one of the worst offenses a business can commit. Other places like China, Russia, the Middle East, and Southwest Asia are more amenable to it, not at all because businesspeople there are criminals. It's just more generally accepted in those cultures. What some might call "bribery", others might call a "service tax", "handling fee" or "entitlement"—in places where it would be strange if you didn't offer such a gratuity to get a deal to the finish line.

I'll be honest: Some people elect not to get into international business after all because they are so uncomfortable with having to face and perhaps get involved in these practices. Bribery is wrong, plain and simple; and dealing with black money promotes tax evasion and degrades the official economy. In fact, there are countries that are so depleted by black money that they can't afford to operate legitimately. This in turn holds the countries back from real economic expansion because other international investors and donors won't go near them, for fear that their money will disappear one day.

When you think about bribery, black money, and other forms of corruption, you probably think of drugs, prostitution, weapons, stolen kidneys, racketeering, bootlegged DVDs, forced labor, etc. It may shock you to hear that instead of all those industries, the field most commonly engaged in corruption worldwide is construction. Think about it: Many construction companies don't just "do work". They are typically contracted to work with raw or finished materials. Think about those materials: Where did they come from? How did they get here? Who produced them? There are so many different layers of business and work in the construction process, from contract awarding to labor to acquisition of materials, that it makes tracing money quite a challenge. In spite of this, there are thousands of perfectly upstanding construction companies who never go near corruption of any kind.

FYI, bribery is most common in countries with a weaker economy, where the government officials and employees don't make a lot of money. Low salaries naturally make corruption more appealing.

You might ask, "But what if I find myself doing business in a place where bribery is expected—where I don't even get a meeting unless I first present a bribe?" This can be sticky. It is then when having a good relationship with a trusted local businessperson can be an invaluable asset. Let that person explain and perhaps handle the situation for you.

A gift is not a bribe. There's nothing wrong with presenting a host with a gift, especially if you're visiting his office. The real difference is what the local government calls it. Sometimes a gift is just a gift; other times, a gift, even if it really is just a gift, is also a bribe. You might test the situation like this: If your host likes the gift so much that he awards you a contract, it may be judged a bribe. So whether your gift is a gift or a bribe, it's most important to know how the country in which you're doing business views the situation.

Another common type of bribery is paying local government officials to expedite legal processes or paperwork to get a deal done faster. There are some places where the local governments will sit on your paperwork until they get their money. So what do you do then? You should act, informed by your own values. One response, if they won't process your paperwork until you pay them under the table, would be to report them to your embassy and let the international commerce folks there sort it out. Another is to pay and move on. I (not-your-mom) can't advise you to just pay them, but I know many companies just pay up and get their business back on track. In fact, some multinational companies have guidelines for gifts and bribes that fit local practices.

In the United States, there are multiple agencies who monitor business operations for acts of corruption. Additionally, the Foreign Corrupt Practices Act was enacted in the United States in 1977 to put an end to companies who had slush (loose cash expense) funds dedicated solely to paying off local officials and politicians. Wherever you do business, be aware that dealing in bribes, black money and similar practices comes loaded with serious risks.

S.G.

Taxes and Regulations at Home and Away

It's exciting to take your business global, but you face complex obligations when you start doing business across borders. Play it safe: Know what you don't know.

YOU PROBABLY SAW the title of this section and said to yourself, "I'm going to skip this one for now and come back to it later, when I'm having trouble falling asleep." You probably thought it would be a whole lot of this:

The organization or reorganization of portions of a multinational enterprise often gives rise to events that, absent rules to the contrary, may be taxable in a particular system. Most systems contain rules preventing recognition of income or loss from certain types of such events. In the simplest form, contribution of business assets to a subsidiary enterprise may, in certain circumstances, be treated as a nontaxable event. Rules on structuring and restructuring tend to be highly complex.

(26 US Code 351)

Fortunately for us both, I'm not going to write like that.

Tax and treaty concepts

Here's the deal. Businesses looking to go international obviously have to pay taxes and abide by regulations, potentially in every country where they operate. Depending on where your business is incorporated, it may have to pay higher or lower taxes than similar companies incorporated elsewhere. Additionally, you may have to pay more or less tax than other companies from your country of origin who do business in countries where you are not active.

To make matters more confusing (sorry), depending on what specific industry you're in, there may be certain tax breaks or exceptions that apply in certain countries only for your industry. The worst case scenario is double taxation, when you pay taxes on the revenue your business earns in the country abroad, plus taxes in your company's home country. Luckily, tax treaties have been widely put in place between countries that trade together, in order to prevent companies who do business internationally from getting smacked with double taxation.

I could yammer on and on about all the different taxation possibilities in all the different countries for all the different types of business sectors, but you would literally die of boredom, old age, or an unfortunate combination of both before I got to the part that fits your specific scenario. So here's what you need to know about international business taxation.

1. You need to consult with a professional accountant who specializes in international business taxation before you set up your business abroad.

2. Your business's taxation scenario is unique, based on, among other things, your country of origin, your business sector, and where you're conducting business (hence, why you need a professional familiar with all those facets to square you away).

3. When conducting international or foreign taxation research, ensure you're researching *corporation* tax information and not *individual* tax information. In many countries, taxation for individuals and businesses differ.

4. The penalties for failing to file international business taxation paperwork and to pay on time are often more expensive than the actual taxes your business will owe.

5. Certain taxation perks and benefits exist, but I'd advise you to be very careful with them (again, hire a professional to prepare your tax filings).

6. The national and international tax regulatory authorities are sharing more data and closing more and more loopholes by the day, swiftly wielding a gigantic hammer of justice on those who defy them. Don't try anything stupid or shady with your business's taxes. It's just not worth it.

Regulations

You want to know something else? I hate regulations. Not because I don't like rules; I love rules. I hate regulations because they make it easy to accidentally get into trouble. It's easy because you never see one regulation walking through the forest by himself. They travel in packs. And while I know they are designed to protect me, my industry, my customers and my livelihood, boy are they hard to read, understand, and apply. Even the people I pay to help me understand regulations hate regulations.

The bad news for those of us just trying to engage morally and ethically in international commerce is that even do-gooders like us get hung up trying to comply with regulations. Similar to taxation, regulations are different based on where you're from and where you want to do business. And since nothing in life is free or easy, if you want to engage in business abroad, it is your responsibility to know, understand and abide by that country's regulations (as well as your own country's regulations).

As you've seen earlier in this book, the most common regulations you're likely to encounter while engaging in international commerce include corruption and trade regulations. Some things that are legal in your country of origin may not be legal in your target market, and vice versa. Additionally, you may not be able to import or export certain items across borders, or the goods you move may need safety tests and certificates that can become very expensive, so do your homework before completing your budgeting and profit calculations. (And by the way, if this isn't enough of a responsibility, you may find that certain *customers* may require certification of workplace safety and pay, environmentally friendly components, and other items—usually at your expense.) That's why it's important to know what regulatory restrictions exist between your country of origin and the countries with which you're planning to conduct business.

Call for help!

The best advice I can give you about complying with international regulations is to understand that you must abide by the regulations of all countries involved, not just your own. You can't just go run and hide under your embassy's skirt if you find yourself in trouble with a foreign nation's regulatory authorities. Your embassy may be able to persuade the foreign government not to chop your hands off, but there are executives who have served time in foreign prisons for not abiding by the regulations imposed by a foreign government.

So how do you play it safe? For both tax and regulation advice, consult with professionals who specialize in international business and trade, and who have experience working with entrepreneurs who have engaged in commerce in the nations in which you're looking to do business.

I sincerely hope I haven't dissuaded you from expanding your business into the international marketplace. It's exciting and very rewarding to take your business global, but it would be a disservice if I didn't make it clear that your responsibilities as a businessperson grow when you're doing business across borders. Just play it safe and work with appropriate professionals to set things up properly, and then be sure to consult with them about obligations you face as your business develops.

S.G.

Nationalization of Businesses

*You may think your business is far too small to
attract a government's attention in this regard.
But if your activity is deemed strategic
to a host government, think twice
and plan ahead.*

NATIONALIZATION IS A CATASTROPHIC BUSINESS EVENT. It happens when a governmental agency takes possession, control and ownership of a private business interest, and may or may not include compensation for the private business. Nationalization is not just the headline-stealing take-over of an oil field by a rogue dictator; it can happen to you. You see it in developing nations as part of regime or political changes, but also quite commonly in industrialized countries. It is also known as reverse privatization.

Eminent Domain/Resumption/Expropriation This happens when private property is taken for public use. The most common form of "nationalization" is eminent domain, used for infrastructure projects like roads or high-tension wires. It is also used when changes in zoning laws require new uses for a particular property. This is an area in which you can be affected drastically, even if you are not operating internationally. New zoning ordinances can restrict the size and type of signage you use, impose obligations to make your business wheelchair accessible, or put you out of business, if for example you own a pub and the property is re-zoned to be alcohol free.

Emergency Industry Nationalization In times of war or catastrophe a government can take control of specific industries, such as airport security following the September 11 attacks in the US or the railroads during World War II in a number of countries.

Corporate Control or Bailout In troubled economic times, governments may step in and prevent a company from failing by taking control of the company or making direct investments into it. This is done because the company is viewed as too critical to fail, due to the product produced or to long-term economic effects. Examples include the British nationalization of Rolls Royce in 1971, or the US bailout of the airline industry.

The laws covering nationalization in industrialized countries are local to the jurisdiction. In developing nations, they could be subject to existing laws or created through political change. Nationalization, the possibility of compensation if it happens, and your rights as a business or property owner are potential major risks you must take into consideration in your business planning, wherever you are located.

M.R.M.

CHAPTER IV

Marketing and Sales

Will They Like Me?

You can learn about the culture, buying trends and lifestyles of your potential customers abroad through a combination of local research, exploration and common sense. Use this information to your advantage... and win.

WHY TO DO WE, AS CONSUMERS, PREFER certain things over other things? What is it about our personal, cultural and aesthetic standards that influences us to like a product or service? These are questions for every entrepreneur around the globe to ponder. Clearly, succeeding in getting consumers in a particular market to like your products or to buy into your offering is central to your success.

All of us are customers. In fact, it's nearly impossible *not* to interact with several businesses or organizations each day. We patronize some businesses for their convenience, pricing or location. We try out new ones based on friendly recommendations. A few earn our hard-earned money based on a solid reputation. Whatever the reason, there are all kinds of factors that contribute to our liking of a particular business.

A sensible approach

First, let's take a look at your business for a moment. We'll set the stage and assume your business is realizing tremendous success in your current market(s). You're achieving top-level sales. Your products and services are incredibly well-received and admired. Your business is cash strong. And now, everything seems to be in place for expansion to a new market, internationally.

Now what? How will you grab some market share in that new location? What can you do to make customers choose you? Do you even remember how you achieved your initial success, in your home market? And if so, will that work in another country nearby, or even halfway around the world?

To start, ask yourself one simple question: *"Does expanding to this particular market make sense?"* At first, it may seem silly to ask it, but think about all the factors that will go into answering it correctly. The best way to do this is to compile a short list of general questions in no particular order that may actually help determine the viability of expansion to the target market(s):

- Do my products or services make sense in this market?

- What is the current appeal of my products there, and will that change over time?

- If so, how long is this trend likely to last, or what is the estimated time-frame for a new trend to take effect?

- Can I change negative perceptions into positive ones, if necessary?

- Is the market on the upswing or downturn, and can it afford my products, based on the economic factors there?

- How have identical or similar products performed in the market?

- What are the current demographics in the area (age, gender, ethnicity, income, etc.), and do they represent a good match for the type of goods or services I will be offering there?

- What are the languages spoken? Will there be a barrier or translation issue with local advertising, marketing, product descriptions, claims or usage?

- Could my products, services or even the marketing/advertising campaigns be construed as offensive or insulting as a result of any religious and/or cultural aspects that might be present?

Take charge of likeability, phase by phase

As we've noted, multiple factors combine in getting a customer to like you. The key will be organizing and managing as many of these elements as possible. You can make it simple and straightforward by dividing activity into three distinct phases. Let's examine them individually.

- **The Awareness phase** There are numerous ways to introduce the arrival of your product or service into a new market. Of course, traditional marketing, advertising and promotion of your offering (or even a specific item) can be implemented in a carefully orchestrated progression. But other formats can be highly effective too (and possibly more successful, early on). Undertakings in product test-marketing such as free crowd sampling, organized focus groups and other means of getting products into the hands of potential customers can be invaluable, because of the immediate reactions and responses that these types of events can convey. If your offering is a service, you might showcase it in free, open demonstrations or special VIP showings to influencers. This is how the awareness of your product begins.

- **The Acknowledgement phase** The return on investments can be huge when you complete the Awareness phase. Reactions from consumers when trying your product will be evident immediately. And the feedback you will receive from focus groups and surveys will be invaluable as well. Those direct responses and opinions from the potential new-market consumers will also go far in telling you what they think of the products and may indicate what they might be willing to pay to obtain them or how far they're willing to travel to purchase them. In short, the acknowledgement segment will begin solidifying their liking (or disliking) of your offerings almost overnight. This data can help shape future advertising and marketing campaigns, which will advance the public awareness of your business and the products it represents in the new market. (Tip: Keep an open mind about the feedback you receive on all fronts. It's possible that not just your marketing but your actual offering could need tailoring, repositioning, or other changes to really succeed.)

- **The Buy-In phase** You've made prospective customers aware you are present. You've showcased your products or services. You received feedback and adjusted accordingly. Now, all that's left is to deliver on your promises and guarantees. This means excellence in customer service, standing behind your products, and becoming a solid member of the business community. Once this is achieved, casual customers will become loyal regulars, and many of them will become raving fans of what you do.

Build on the foundation

As a small business owner, it will always be important to remember your customers will still need to *like* the things you offer in order to fully engage with them. This likeability factor is what keeps them coming back. It's also what prompts fans to recommend you to others. And once the word about your offering has gotten around in a positive way, your business becomes identifiable on numerous levels as a trusted source in your new market abroad… and you discover that you have created the foundation for a robust brand.

M.P.

Brand, Language, Color and Market Dress in Target Markets

*You might not think it's necessary to consider
changes in how you go to market abroad,
compared with in your home territories.
But successful entrepreneurs do.*

THE FACE THAT YOUR PRODUCT OR SERVICE PRESENTS in your target market can make or break your business abroad. Unless you or members of your team thoroughly know the target market's culture and language, you will probably need some outside help from knowledgeable advisors and potential customers to make sure you put your best foot forward. This section will help you organize your thinking so you can ask good questions and make smart choices, given the answers you receive.

Branding—do you need to put on a new face?

Hopefully you have developed a brand in your home market and it's working well for you. Depending on your target market, it could work fine abroad. Or it could be disastrous. The biggest corporations in the world are not immune from brand blunders, so take this issue seriously, even if your company is a one-person band.

Some brands work well without a bit of adaptation. Singer sewing machines, Black & Decker tools, airlines, pharmaceutical companies and many others maintain their branding without change worldwide. But you can be sure that this consistency is not due to whimsical thinking. Unvarying global brands have survived very careful testing and scrutiny.

Other giants wisely massage their brands for certain target markets. One of the most-reported examples of brand adaptation comes from Coca Cola. If you simply search for characters that make the sound of "Coca Cola" in Chinese, the meaning of those characters is either "female horse stuffed with wax" or, more famously, "bite the wax tadpole." Neither of these images makes you want to reach for a cold drink. So the Coke team adapted the brand name to sound like "kekou kele," which fortunately means "let your mouth rejoice." In the auto industry, that kind of mistake, not caught in time, proved costly. Ford introduced a vehicle into Spanish-speaking countries named the Fiera. However, in many Spanish dialects, *fiera* means *ugly shrew*. As you can imagine, the car did not sell very well under that name.

Obviously, the more you can keep your branding unified in all your markets, the better. Sometimes a brand's modification that works well elsewhere can even lead to changing your original brand at home to match. Think of the Kentucky Fried Chicken franchise, second in sales to McDonalds in the fast-food world now. As the company grew beyond its Kentucky, US roots, it came to be known worldwide as simply KFC, and its logo portrait of Colonel Sanders, based on the original founder Harland Sanders, has been modified with time. Now, KFC can offer non-chicken meals anywhere in the world without any brand confusion. In China, where it's the largest fast food chain, the menu includes tree fungus salad and rice congee, among other local dishes. It's likely that the millions of KFC customers around the world have no idea what KFC originally stood for, and that's fine with Yum! Brands, KFC's parent company. (Notice that the name Yum! is a smart international food chain branding choice itself.)

It could be that neither of these strategies—adapting or staying globally consistent—is best for your company as it expands internationally. Depending on your business's overall international strategy, you might even enter a foreign market under a new or shared brand. If you are partnering with a local company that has an established, respected brand, it might suit your products or services to market them under the local company's brand. Or you can invest in developing a local brand that's all your own. This may require a lot of resources and time, but it's worth weighing against your other options.

Language challenges

The world is littered with hilarious, ribald, or downright weird translations of names, job titles, signs, instructions and so forth, as any traveler can tell you. You don't want your best efforts to launch your offerings in a new territory to be noted first as a good laugh. Consider a few unfortunate tries:

- A ramen instant soup: Soup for Sluts—Cheap, Fast and Easy

- A main dish: Meat Muscle Stupid Bean Sprouts

- A snack: Inca Chips—Ethnican Flavor

- A treat: Gelatinous Mutant Coconut Candy

- Some signs: Racist Park (with arrow), Slip and Fall Down Carefully (with Olympic-style icons showing people who weren't careful), Please Don't Touch Yourself / Let Us Help You to Try Out / Thanks! (presumably, in a grocery or china store)

- A sticker on a coffee carafe: Be careful of children when inning hot liquids

These blunders happen when entrepreneurs (and even some industry giants and governments) put together messages in English, dictionary in hand but minus quality control. Mistakes can happen in any translation, so get the best translator you can find, preferably local and familiar with your industry. Test the translations he or she produces on potential users or buyers before you commit to producing marketing tools using them. And triple proofread every word and triple check every graphic.

Also, be warned: you can make gaffes and lose face or business even when you share a language with the target country. Just ask any Spaniard who has attempted to market in South American countries, or a French Canadian who wants to sell in France, or any of the English-based entrepreneurs who unknowingly assume their English-based target market speaks and writes exactly as they do.

All of this applies equally to your instructions on packages, brochures, ads, websites and so forth—wherever you connect verbally with your target market. And in that regard, make sure you are fully aware of any obligations to present information in multiple languages. Consumer products' packages and user manuals across Europe are crammed with mouse-type texts saying the same thing in ALL the languages where they are sold.

Color associations and design considerations

Colors spark feelings and moods, as everyone knows. But the meanings we associate with colors follow culturally specific patterns. As you plan your marketing and packaging materials for a target market, don't assume that the associations you attach to a color will hold true in your target market. For example, McDonalds had to adjust their marketing campaign in Japan because their mascot, Ronald McDonald, a clown with a painted white face, received a very negative reception there. Painted white faces are associated with death in the Japanese culture. The chart opposite gives you an example of the wildly varying associations that different cultures make for just the color red.

Cultural Color Meanings of Red*

Western: energy, excitement, action; danger; love, passion; a warning to stop; anger; Christmas, when combined with green; Valentine's Day

Eastern: prosperity; good fortune; worn by brides; symbol of joy when combined with white

Jewish culture: sacrifice, sin

Christian culture: sacrifice, passion, love

China: the color of good luck and celebration; vitality, happiness, long life; used as a wedding color; used in many ceremonies from funerals to weddings; used for festive occasions; traditionally worn on Chinese New Year to bring luck and prosperity

India: color of purity, fertility, love, beauty; wealth, opulence and power; used in wedding ceremonies; a sign of a married woman; also color of fear and fire

Thailand: color for Sunday

Japan: life, anger and danger

Cherokee Nation: success, triumph

Aboriginal Australians: represents the land and earth, a ceremonial color

South Africa: color of mourning

Nigeria: usually reserved for ceremonies, worn by chiefs

Russia: associated with the Bolsheviks and Communism, means *beautiful* in Russian language, often used in marriage ceremonies

In addition to considering these symbolic associations, pay attention to both the color palette and color combinations that are favored in your target market. For example, a slightly fluorescent cast in colors is popular in some countries, while in others you might see a predominance of brilliant reds, pinks and purples with gold accents.

It's also important to get a feel for the local design preferences in your sector. Many American entrepreneurs prepare their product presentation materials, meet with a local buyer, and hear the familiar soft rejection, "I love it but it looks too American." It's often hard to get the buyer to describe just what that means, but it definitely means the buyer has a solid reason to refuse to buy. If you can, try to partner with such buyers to develop a look that overrides this rejection. Or work with local designers.

Of course, the opposite can be true—think about how US-made blue jeans were prized in communist countries, not that long ago.

*The chart above is slightly edited and is included here with permission from its author, Judy Scott-Kemmis. For further details and other colors, visit http://www.empower-yourself-with-color-psychology.com/cultural-color.html

The best way to educate yourself about these things is to scout out your competition's market dress and sales collateral, whether in person or online. Once you get sensitized to these elements, you can decide how much you want to localize colors and design matters in your own materials. The point is to be strategic about it.

Size, use and price patterns

There are other, subtle things you'll want to check out in your target market. Consider these intriguing examples:

- Japanese apartments and homes are very compact and short on storage space. If you export books that are too big to fit on relatively shallow Japanese book shelves, they will go unsold—not necessarily because they are bad products, or undesirable, but because they simply fall off the shelves, or are too big to even fit in.

- Do-it-yourself tool importers face real challenges in Italy, because so many people live in apartments where a) they do very little DIY and thus don't dream of a workshop full of shiny tools, and b) they don't have space to store many tools, even if they are such dreamers.

- Certain over-the-counter medicines, for example aspirin, are sold as quite expensive preparations in some countries, quite unlike the bulk bottles of 100 or 200 tablets you encounter in the US.

- In India, entrepreneurs have made fortunes by repackaging shampoo and similar products in single-use packets and selling them at newsstands and via hand carts. This makes them affordable for huge numbers of people with very low incomes, since they can pay as they go, buying at a low price only when they need the product, vs. investing in a large bottle at a much higher price.

In situations like these, reformatting (printing your books in smaller dimensions), or localizing your product offering (a compact tool box meant for normal household repairs, not DIY projects), or offering what the public expects (small packets of aspirin or personal care items) can open opportunities you might have missed, if you didn't know about the market dress and consumer preferences in play.

It's true that the world is shrinking and we all are more aware and accepting of the ways other cultures live and think, and that trend can be a real benefit to your global expansion plans. Just don't make assumptions about other markets—find out what's what. You are not obliged to go native, but you do want to be smart.

K.S. and M.R.M.

Localization vs. Straightforward Import/Export

If you want to expand your product or service line internationally, be prepared to localize it, to give it the best possible chance of selling.

IT'S AMAZING TO SEE how uniquely different countries in the world are. People speak different languages, love totally different music and art, wear clothes that are unbelievably different in styles and colors, bring up their children according a huge range of values and beliefs, and cook with the broadest range of tastes, techniques and ingredients you can imagine. So as an entrepreneur, how do you market products or services to people so uniquely different? You have to drill down to the lowest common denominator and start your marketing calculus there (and for the record, this is why even if you are a high-tech, gung-ho business enthusiast, at least one Humanities or Cultural Awareness class won't kill you).

Basic or niche?

What do all people like? They like to eat. They like to drink. They like to laugh and smile. They like to look and feel good. They like to feel loved. They like to feel smart. They like to feel needed and uplifted or improved. They love their children and want them to be happy and to succeed. When we start listing these traits that people like to have and be, it's not so hard to think about concepts that appeal to almost all people. If your offering falls into that realm, you're in luck. You still may have work to do to sell them abroad, but you are closer to fulfilling basic needs and that's a bonus.

But what if your product or service is extremely niche (say, it's powder that prevents foot odor, or it's an adventure travel agency)? Right away you can rule out countries where bare feet or sandals are the standard, or where the local economy will not support your valuable booking service.

So let's assume you've already designed a product or service for one market, and you think it has a chance of succeeding in another market. Now *that's* a relevant and realistic problem!

Change for the good

Well, you have two options, which fortunately you can take in two stages. You can import your product as is (or nearly as is) to markets that you believe will easily accept and purchase it. For instance, if you have a US-based children's rocking horse company and you do well in the United States, you could very likely see a decent amount of success marketing it as is to English-language markets like England, Canada, Australia and New Zealand (though your rocking horses' names might vary with the market and your marketing and packaging will need Anglicizing). Then, with some new packaging and translation, you could add profits in non-English speaking Western Europe as well. Eventually, however, you'll likely reach a point where you can't profitably market your product to other markets *as is,* due to cultural constraints.

At that point, if your research supports your appetite for risk, you can move into your second option, localization. As we have seen, localization is simply adapting your product or service to appeal to new markets. The adaptation could include adjusting the product or service's look, positioning, target audience, etc. to attune to language, cultural, political, or legal characteristics. Perhaps if you change the rocking horse to a rocking camel or giraffe, you can open entirely new markets. Or maybe you need to add a little story book to your rocking creature's package, to explain the notion of rocking critters and engage parents and children in a new tradition. As you go through this process, look for windfall bonuses: Your localization process could very possibly yield products or services that will be uniquely attractive back in your home market. Look for chances to check that out back home, once you have some localized product to test. Those rocking camels and giraffes might become the latest craze.

Cautious optimism and pragmatic realism

Be careful not to assume your dream scenario of sales abroad will play out in reality, localized or not. Chances are, if you produce a perfume made from rattlesnake venom, you will have to make some adjustments to your perfume's chemical composition before you can market it all over the world. There just isn't enough venom to go around. Make those adjustments, however, and your perfume can now be marketed elsewhere. Or, as a more practical example, if you have an internet-based business, but your website can only be viewed in Arabic, you'll want to translate your website for other global languages to attract more business internationally.

Here's a real-world example: Back in the 1990s, Land Rover imported the Defender sport utility vehicle to the United States. Its rugged design, powerful engine, and unmatched off-road capability naturally (or ironically) appealed to urban-dwelling, predominantly highway-traveling Americans. Bottom line: The Defender's success was awesome. However, in 1998 the US Department of Transportation changed certain regulations that would have required extensive adjustments to the Defender's production. After conducting a cost-benefit analysis, Land Rover decided that it simply wasn't cost-effective to localize and re-tool the Defender to meet the new United States regulations. Sadly, as a result, 1997 was the last model year of the Defender in the United States. The moral of the story is that sometimes, localization just isn't worth the cost, even though the product might sell reasonably well.

Where to start the localization process

If you want to attract more customers internationally, you will probably eventually have to localize to some degree. The greatest drawback to localization is the cost. It costs money to adapt anything. To rebuild and host a website in another language costs money. To adapt marketing and product packaging in another language costs money. Even if you plan to run the cost-benefit analysis and conduct a regional market test yourself, that takes time, and time costs money! However, there are right and wrong ways to do everything, including localization.

You may recall that in our *Starting a Business* book, we point out that the safest way to start a new business is to "moonlight", to start building a new business slowly and inexpensively at night or on the weekends, while you still have your current job. This alleviates much of the risk you would face if you just quit your job, took out loans, and dove right into the deep end of entrepreneurship.

The safest way to initiate a localization plan is very similar to moonlighting. You start the research process yourself and expand into other markets gradually, starting with markets that are most similar to your own. For example, if you own a company that is headquartered in upstate New York that manufactures and installs custom residential vertical blinds, and you decide you want to expand internationally, a logical and seamless first step would obviously be Yemen, due to all the cultural similarities. Just kidding, try Canada. Canada is a common first step for a United States company looking to dip a toe into the international business arena, due to the multitude of cultural similarities Americans share with Canadians. If you are sensitive to the complex issues of English and French markets within Canada, you have an even greater advantage.

Western European entrepreneurs have similar advantages in expanding within Europe, due to the close geographical proximity of many countries, and the high percentage of multi-lingual citizens in them. Additionally, while cultures differ among the European countries, people generally share an awareness and understanding of diverse cultures there. Still, history, language, long-term ties and animosities, stereotypes and a host of other factors make this a fascinating but challenging area in which to go international.

When to stop?

Depending on your offering, by embracing localization, you might be able to eventually market your product or service to the entire world. The real question is: Is it worth it? It's impressive if you can say that you sell your product on every continent (except Antarctica). But when it boils down to the bottom-line profit, you may find that once you get to a certain level of global expansion, it may not be worth the expense and trouble to adapt a product or service for those remaining, markedly different cultures, or for cultures in which your offering is a non-starter. Don't take that personally. Let the facts direct your expansion and play to win.

S.G.

Building a Brand and Making It Work

A brand is not created overnight, and not every business sets out to make one. But following these simple guidelines can help your business become the brand leader.

DEPENDING ON THE TYPE OF BUSINESS YOU OPERATE, a *brand* can represent a multitude of things to the buying public. Often, it's the actual name of a business. In other cases, it can be a certain niche or specific product a company has created. It can even be a recognizable logo, an image or symbol that, over time, becomes synonymous with the overall profile and success of your operation. Whatever it is, the goal for your brand should be to identify your products and services as distinct from those of other sellers in the same market. The international business question then is: Should you bring your brand from your home country, or adapt or create a new one in the target market?

Brand basics

First, what actually constitutes a brand? It's a wide-ranging sum of positive experiences your customers have (or will have) with your business and the products and services you offer. And the stronger your brand becomes, the better it will communicate what your company does for your customers (your messaging), how you do it (your process), and at the same time, establish confidence and credibility (your track record). Once established, you can use your brand extensively in business promotion and outreach, in marketing and advertising campaigns. It can help you gain and control market share. It can eventually become the public identity of your business (think Coke or MasterCard).

Start from scratch... again

So, how do you get started, creating and then building your brand identity in your target market abroad? Note that even if your brand has been successful in your home market, given a different culture, a different currency, and quite possibly, different buying trends and habits in your new market, that brand might have zero power and appeal. Test it out on all parties important to your success: customers, the competition, marketing channels, buyers, sales reps, etc.

If you find that your brand is a bad fit, it may be smart to start from scratch, rather than adapt your branding from home. Before moving forward, look into the past to see what might be the best starting point for recreating your initial successes. Look around you now, in the present, and see if any trends in the target market prompt a new idea. Finally, look to the future—are there any developments on the horizon that you can capitalize on and surge *ahead* of the competition?

If you're still a little unsure as to where you might begin, here are some thoughts that will help to ensure your basic groundwork is on track. Let's start with a vital Step One.

Your value proposition

The first item you must tackle is to create and clearly define a value proposition for the new market you are entering. This step represents a promise of value to be delivered to your customers and a promise of quality that your business will stand behind. This proposition, which is not to be mistaken with the pricing of your products and services, begins the process of establishing your overall brand. It will also begin a comparison that will differentiate you from the competition. The value proposition you create can and should be updated on a regular basis too: it should reflect new products, ideas and philosophies you have instilled as part of your operation and culture. So just like a business plan, your value proposition should be reviewed often.

Consider for example that the Hello Kitty line of toys and accessories is typically aimed at little girls in Japan, North America and western Europe. In China, Hello Kitty watches are a hot item for twenty-something women. Their owners are viewed as hip, trendy, with-it. Who would have thunk it? This successful rebranding was the fruit of flexible, open-minded thinking. If the Hello Kitty folks had doggedly (sorry about that) targeted little Chinese girls, they would have missed a major opportunity.

After your value proposition is clear and aligned with your target market's conditions, you can proceed to brand establishment. The points below will help you highlight key aspects and philosophies of your business. They help support the very value proposition you are broadcasting to your current and potential customers.

- **Clearly define what you do**. Make sure every potential customer knows what business you're in, what you have to offer and how it will benefit them. Constantly review what's going on with your target audience, check the fit of your product and service offerings to it, and then alter any aspects of your marketing and advertising to match. By delivering a clear message to prospects about who you are, where you are located, and what you have to offer, you make a strong initial case for people to do business with you. This is how a brand is born.

- **Be identifiable**. The new value proposition, your logo and colors, your goods or services, your business model, and the market niche you service all help shape the identity of your business, through increasing familiarity. This is especially important when expanding to an international market.

- **Be different**. Look for ways to differentiate yourself from others in your market category. This can happen on countless fronts. *Different* could simply mean you are better than your competitors. But you may also offer higher quality, a better price/value ratio, a bigger selection, better customer service, a better location, or more innovative solutions. You get the idea: A differentiator could be as simple as your operating hours. If they are different from traditional ones, you'll stand out (but first confirm with the appropriate authority that you can vary them). Defining your business offering as unique (and showcasing it) gives off a great vibe, gets prospects' attention, and give you the opportunity to convert them to customers.

- **Give your brand an image.** That image might be you, as the owner, interacting on a daily basis with customers. It could be your employees, delivering killer service without fail. It could be the incredible product guarantees you maintain. Whatever you pick will be the initial focal point in the value proposition you established in the new chosen market. It must be clear, concise and completely believable. The image you forge will deliver positive word-of-mouth referrals and develop a positive mindset toward your company in the local community.

- **Give back**. Ensuring your business is active in the local community wherever you are located is vital for your brand *and* your image. No matter what direction you take (charitable giving, sponsoring events, volunteer work, etc.), your brand stands to benefit from your generosity and service ethic as well. Your good deeds will be favorably associated with the quality of your business.

- **Be consistent and deliver a better experience every time**. Ensure that every staff member (should you have any) acts as your brand ambassador. Think about the tone you and your staff communicate to your customers. Also think like your target audience. What will resonate and compel them to buy into your brand?

- **Build in measurements.** Establish budgets and financial targets and to manage and evaluate how well your brand strategy feeds into your various product categories. How will you know you've succeeded, if you don't establish goals and mileposts up front?

Putting the pieces together

It's important to understand that creating a brand in your new market abroad may not be immediately vital to initial success. In fact, countless businesses achieve financial prosperity and experience rapid growth without paying attention to branding. It's true that a business could even sell its products or services with minimal to moderate success, and continue that course of action perpetually, without brand development. However, long-term financial success, which will represent the overall sustained monetary value of your company, will primarily rely upon a particular facet of your success (products, service, experience, etc.) or even a combination of them. That's why many businesses decide to create a visible presence suggesting a widespread, positive consumer experience in their brand identity.

So the moral of this story (and your ultimate goal) is to create a business brand in your target market that vividly portrays a rock-solid value proposition. Showcase this proposition through your marketing, advertising and outreach and allow it to evolve into a long-term reputation, to the point that your customers are compelled to share their positive experiences with your organization with others. That's when the brand-building process really begins to deliver.

M.P.

Pricing and Business Models

Here's a dose of reality you should take
before leaping into business abroad.

THERE ARE MULTITUDES OF WAYS you can structure your business to reduce product and distribution costs and operating expenses. But, just as with your domestic business, it really comes down to what makes the most sense for your particular product or service and market area abroad. However, even if your initial, long-term goal is to grow into a model that utilizes products and services from all over the globe, it isn't necessary to start that way.

Building a better mouse trap, in stages

Many small businesses start with basic business models as they gear up to provide their "mouse trap" to customers in their local area. This can be helpful when you are still trying to build your brand, determine the viability of a product or service and to prove the concept to others, including investors. Once you have a business that is self-sustaining and generating revenue, however, it's a good idea to begin revisiting the different elements of the business to identify where you can create efficiencies, how to reduce major cost centers and how to grow the revenue of your business. These are great ways to use the resources that are already available to further enhance your balance sheet.

So what follows is going to seem like I'm throwing cold water on your plans to get into international business. Read on and consider how points below might apply to you.

The trap part of your mousetrap's model

What happens all too often is that business owners try to apply what they know to be true generally about their industry's products or services and its processes, and it sets them on a path that they cannot afford. I know, it's fun to dream, but you have to start small and focus on the core business. Get customers, make sales and turn a profit. The other activities and focuses can bog you down to the point where you're spending all your time worrying about things that haven't happened yet in an effort to combat every shortcoming that you foresee. This stage can be deadly for an entrepreneur, because the business can grow stagnant while every pea on the plate gets analyzed and forward momentum stalls out.

I know this flies in the face of what most people were taught, but it's the way the real world works. Only in textbooks is time, money, the cost of money and credibility theoretical. You can spend an eternity working and reworking your strategic plan until it's perfect and you get an "A" on your homework. But the real world is hard on dreamers. I see it every day: great ideas, smart people—but spinning their wheels until they burn out, taking along their supporters. The business either gets shelved, shuts down or flames out.

A friend once said that until you get to the equivalent of ten million dollars per year in revenue, you have a hobby, not a business. That may be a little extreme, and there is nothing wrong with having a small business that is profitable, but the moral of the story is to get your business going and start making some money, *then* worry about how you can leverage technologies and the global economy to maximize the results of your activities.

Getting real about theoretical "improvements"

Think about this: What if you have a start-up in the US that is bringing in $50,000-$100,000 per year and your current cost of goods (COG) is 35 per cent of your total revenue. You think that by spending thousands of dollars and hundreds of hours, you could reduce the cost of your products by 15 per cent.

Let's check that out. At $100,000 revenue, you would have $35,000 in product cost. Say the improvements would save you $5,250 over the course of 12 months. That's $437.50 per month, or around $14.00 per day. Now, what would have a greater impact on your business: finding ways to save, or going out and getting MORE Business, MORE customers, etc.?

In contrast, think about a ten-million dollar per year operation. You would have $350,000 in COG and you would be saving $52,500 annually. Now that's a number worth considering. That's the fully loaded cost of an employee whose job could be to identify, implement and track efficiency opportunities for the business. Which one sounds like a better plan? At the risk of being repetitive, let me say that the first and highest hurdle of a small business is to get off the ground high enough that you actually have a cash-flow positive operation. Get there first and don't get hung up on all of the fun analysis paralysis and research. Once you're there, *then* go back and improve on your business, once all of the facts are in and you have the appropriate historical data to make impactful decisions.

The value of international business

This can add a level of complexity to a business that most entrepreneurs don't see in their day-to-day lives. Have you ever wondered why soft drinks are only a few pennies in some countries and over $1.00 in others? When companies get large enough to operate in multiple countries, it can become difficult to find viable sources for resources at price points that work with the local economy. If you want to make an audio speaker, for example, you may have to source raw materials from local suppliers and use local labor to manufacture your product, in order to make it affordable in that specific market area. You also may have to change the materials or ingredients to maintain cost-effective manufacturing and reach the wholesale or retail price point the local marketplace needs.

Let's assume that you are a manufacturer based in the United States and you are located in a state with a strong labor union presence. So it would be impractical for you to hire non-union employees. Also, let's pretend that your company manufactures table lamps, and these lamps are built from materials that are sourced from suppliers who are also located in the United States. Now, you might have high quality US steel, brass, glass and wiring all being assembled by union factory workers at, let's say, $20 per hour. Plus, you have to gross that number up for all of the benefits, contributions, health care and other insurance. So you really have $30 per hour in line labor. If the average table lamp requires $15 in materials and two hours of labor ($60), then you would have a raw cost of $75, not including packaging, quality control and other peripheral items.

What if you decided to start building and selling similar lamps in Vietnam? First, you could use lower-cost metals, since the market is more competitive and the material specifications are often different. Also, the same two hours of shop labor would only cost around $2.50. So if the materials could be acquired for 33 per cent less and the labor was $2.50, then the same lamp in theory could be manufactured for $12.50. In this model, you could export the lamp to the country that represents your largest customer base and sell it for much less, with even better gross margins.

Finally, remember not to automatically discount your products or services based on what you've seen in the market abroad. If what you offer is truly unique, then people will pay. Period. Think about all of the oddball items, custom services, luxury goods, technology, specialty retail products, etc. that you may have bought in the past. People will pay surprising prices if it's something they haven't seen, or it's something they need, or if their friends, family and coworkers don't have it (or conversely, if they *all* have it). Once you establish your business and can be fairly confident in its future, that's the best time to go out and try to find ways to reduce cost and make the offerings more affordable for a larger market.

M.O.

CHAPTER V

Logistics, Travel

When to Go There, When Not

*Although it may seem that airport hopping means
your business has really made it, it can really
cost you... in more ways than one.*

I STILL REMEMBER my first big international business trip. It was exciting on
so many levels. I felt like I was finally really part of the global marketplace. I'd
worked years to sit in that business class seat and truly belong. Before that moment, I felt I was just acting the part.

Many other (typically, young) professionals feel the same way about flying long distances for business. They may act cool, but inside they feel like big
players in the game of global commerce. And they believe that their work, measured purely by the distance they travel to conduct it, will produce positive results,
because now they're one of the guys and gals who go on the big trips.

I can tell you the very last thing on my mind during my first business trip
abroad was whether it was really necessary. I was thrilled, and just assumed I
needed to go. The decision to send me was made at some level above my head,
and I figured that because it was made, I had to (and got to) go. As an employee,
your job is to do whatever your bosses tell you to do, right? But looking back,
years later, I know I didn't really *need* to make that trip. I could have easily conducted those meetings via video teleconference.

The good (?) old days

In the old days of international business, when you wanted a face-to-face
meeting, whether it was initial or routine, you had very few options: either you
went to them, they came to you, or you met at some mutually inconvenient place
elsewhere. Nowadays, however, things have changed. While not actually physically getting smaller, the business world has gotten *a lot* smaller. By walking into
another room or making a simple phone call, we can visually connect with practi-

cally anyone in the world, certainly anyone with a cell phone or Internet connection. In fact, with services like Skype™ or others, we can even do it for *FREE*. With connections as convenient and affordable as these, even traditionalists conduct business the new way most of the time.

For the sake of illustration, let's say you're thinking about going halfway around the world for two weeks (two days of travel on both sides, and ten days of scheduled meetings, non-essential tours of your customer's facilities, etc.). You're probably thinking,

> *Of course I would love a good reason to travel abroad, and I know it would be great for my business partner and me to meet our current and prospective customers and vendors in their home country, face-to-face. But when I ran the numbers, it will cost us $30,000 in expenses to go there for two weeks. So how do I determine whether we should actually go?*

Don't worry, this won't be a finance lesson, but let me help put things in perspective. I can't tell you what to do, of course, but I would advise you think about these factors when making your decision.

What exactly are you trying to accomplish?

Let's get real. You should be able to clearly state what you want as outcomes, and where numbers are involved, you should be able to calculate and defend them. Some typical goals include these:

- Scouting the market; attending a trade show or expo

- Meeting with a slate of potential partners, hires, vendors, etc.

- Negotiating a complex agreement

- Presenting your future line of products or services for input and feedback

- Selling/buying

- Sorting out problems, building trust

- Soothing hurt feelings or untangling misunderstandings

- Celebrating mutual successes

- Winding down a relationship, amicably or otherwise

- Sourcing replacements for current partners or checking out additional ones

To some extent you can put a price tag on the benefits of your trip and a percentage of success you think you'll achieve for the more intangible goals.

Do you really need to go?

Be honest with yourself, now. Will your relationship with the customer fail, or will the deal not get done if you do not physically go? If you think the customer might not take you seriously if you don't come in person, I'd advise you to think again. That may have been the case thirty years ago, but today, we all have access to the same technology and we really can talk face to face electronically. Depending on the size of the deal, your customer might even respect your fiscal responsibility for electing not to come in person, if the cost of the trip places significant pressure on the deal. Which leads me to my next point...

Will the benefit or profit outweigh the cost(s) of the trip?

This may have made you smirk, and I hope it did. If it stung a bit, know that you're not alone. I know there's a decent chance this has happened to you—when the cost of the trip wound up being more than what you earned from the deal. This is a classic entrepreneurial growing pain, and you live and learn. And in all fairness, sometimes you have to travel to learn what a bad deal you almost signed up for.

Numerous entrepreneurs, after traveling halfway across the world to do an international deal for their small business, actually lose money when the cost/benefit hashes out in the end. They realize that it actually cost them more to travel abroad than what the bottom-line profits from the deal yielded. As a rule of thumb, cost out the trip ahead of time, and if you're not netting at least a 10-20% bottom-line profit, either find a way to do the trip more cheaply, or just don't go.

Of course you'll know best how to judge the intangibles. If you're traveling to meet a potential investor who is seriously considering making a $5 million investment in your small business, I would say it's definitely worth making the trip to shake his hand and look him in the eye.

What about the home front costs?

Here's something else to keep in mind about weighing the cost/benefit of a business trip abroad: What is happening at your home office while you're out of the country for a week or more? Is business being conducted as usual? If you know you'll experience a drop in business or miss foreseeable opportunities while you're away, you need to take that into consideration as well. Bottom line: remember that at the end of the day, businesses are in business to *make* money, not *lose* money.

The benefit of a cost/benefit focus

You'll notice a recurring theme here centered on cost/benefit—whether the benefit you see after doing something makes its cost worth it. Cost/benefit can be analyzed to infinite levels, and while this may tip your decision-making scale regarding your next big trip, it likely won't change the outcome if you're a small business. That's because it's much easier to track cost/benefit on a small business scale.

Looking back to my first trip, I see now why so many other young professionals felt like I did. They were so excited about playing a role in the fancy-sounding global marketplace that they didn't even notice certain details. In the process, they spent 22 hours in a cramped seat (twice!), lost luggage, stayed in a crummy hotel, and felt mostly horrible from jetlag, language fog, unidentifiable foods and unfamiliar customs. Then, just when they were getting partially adjusted, flying home and spending the next week digging out inboxes and trying to get back to normal. The glory of global business.

In the case of my first big trip, all of this really didn't matter in the long run, because everyone got what they wanted. But I suppose it could have turned out badly too. My bosses sent me over because they could get me there and back on a budget that made the trip worth it, while a firm handshake and easy smile represented the company in person. A win-win for all, luckily.

S.G.

Delivery Systems and Processes

It's plain good sense to explore all the options you have for delivering your product or service.

THE NATURE OF DELIVERING goods and services in our ever-growing global marketplace is very dynamic. It wasn't too long ago that products would simply be manufactured, packaged, palletized, shipped, warehoused and inventoried. Or you'd set up a foreign office and start delivering your service. Boom. Done. Back then, the sales and marketing team of an organization would go about promoting and selling products to their target market and the inventory levels would be monitored. When reorders or restocks took place, the supply chain warehouse team or service provider team would facilitate those needs, using KANBAN or SAP technology, and that was it. But now we live in a world where most of the products and services that are designed, developed, produced and sold are sourced from all corners of the globe in an effort to compete and stay profitable against competitors.

By doing some very basic research and analysis, an entrepreneur can identify certain competitive advantages that exist based on geographic areas, economic strengths or weaknesses, distances from other parts of their supply chain, etc. These types of advantages help businesses create operational efficiencies in regard to labor, materials, costs and timelines. However, making strategic maneuvers in these areas can bring on the need for additional resources not found in the traditional production and distribution model.

Trading companies

For example, let's consider trading companies. Their purpose is to help identify needs in a local country, communicate effectively with the resources being utilized there for producing, shipping, handling logistics and managing any other necessary paperwork that may be unique to a country or area of the world. Their advantages far outweigh their expense, in my humble opinion. It would take me hours if not days and weeks to fully research and brief myself on every nuance of doing business in another country.

Unfortunately, there are a few common disadvantages and costs that come along with trading companies' services. Sometimes the trading company isn't the most ethical. You may find that they are not necessarily working in a fiduciary capacity for you and your organization (looking out for your best interests), but are actually steering you and the business you bring to certain providers, based on other arrangements they have with them—referral fees, bribes and other perks. Consider for example the concierge at a hotel. You would hope that she is sending you to restaurants that are truly the best choice for you, based on the parameters you give (say, a cozy local bistro). However I've seen too often that these individuals send people to certain places in exchange for gift cards, cash, and other perks.

To be fair, this is unfortunate only if the concierge's suggestions are not great. Recently, the people I was traveling with really wanted to have an Italian dinner. So naturally we asked the concierge for help. We were quickly directed to a particular restaurant. There we were served some of the worst Italian food I've ever eaten. Needless to say, that restaurant is no longer in business. But at other times, I've been wildly impressed by a concierge's choice. Then I go out of my way to find her and offer an appropriate gratuity. Anyway, my point is that a reputable, ethical trading company will provide a ton of valuable insight and perform countless tasks to expedite your needs for between 3 and 7 per cent of your bill, depending on the country, the size of the workload given *them* and whether or not you represent repeat business for *them*. For a one-time project, expect to pay more.

Since trading companies tend to specialize in goods, you may not find them engaged in facilitating services you need to deliver the services you in turn sell. However, in that case, you might find a retired professional, a consultant, a person who was recently laid off or someone else who can advise you or actually handle your activity in the target market. The same caution about ethical practices applies, however.

Drop shipping and consignment

Another popular method of delivering products to the marketplace is to drop ship.

Drop shipping means the products leave directly from the manufacturer's or distributor's warehouse and go straight to the end user. Often this is the case with web-based, e-commerce businesses that run virtually and with very little overhead. This is why they can survive on nominal margins, and why consumers typically find the lowest prices for the goods they are seeking online.

Consignment is another interesting concept, in that it requires you to hold inventory on behalf of a client at your cost, or to be prepared to accept unsold goods returned for full credit. This type of arrangement is most common in large-scale distribution relationships such as with manufacturers and "big-box" retailers or hypermarkets. These retailers often represent such huge volumes of business that they can control the terms of product placement, availability and distribution. That is why many big-box operations rely on tens of thousands of manufactures and distributors at all times. It's a way for them to ensure that they are getting the best pricing, purchasing requirements, payment terms, etc.

Orders from these giants are very exciting and appealing to a small business because they do often represent significant top-line revenue and volume. And that usually allows for expansion of facilities and staff for the small business. However, you have to be careful. Just remember, revenue doesn't necessarily mean profit. Often, the competitiveness of these buyers will drive prices down to the point where you are making such narrow margins that you can only justify it in terms of exposing your product or brand and to move volume to gain larger-scale production runs of a product or product line. It's still with the smaller retailers and direct selling activities where you will make the majority of your profit. The last thing you want is to expand your infrastructure and inventory, only to accommodate one customer who can leave at any time or dump the majority of stock you shipped originally back on you. Believe me, sometimes they do, and that can bankrupt a business almost immediately. Just to be clear, these types of relationships aren't necessarily bad. As an entrepreneur and small business owner, you just need to understand all facets of the deal and make decisions based on your own particular read on the situation.

Crystal ball gazing

As we roll further into the 21st century, it's becoming more and more common for the things consumers are buying to be delivered electronically, especially with cloud-based storage capabilities, high-speed data delivery, Content Delivery Networks (CDNs) and free Wi-Fi almost everywhere. These types of businesses can be fun because they often carry extremely low costs of goods. Therefore you can do much better financially on a lot less revenue than with a traditional brick and mortar business saddled with serious fixed overhead expenses. The next wave of cost savings is already coming from the ever-growing use of robotics and 3-D printing. It seems that in the not too distant future, most of the consumer goods we buy will be delivered on the same day we order. So keep pushing the envelope, at home and in your target markets abroad, and try to identify where you and your business can benefit.

M.O.

CHAPTER VI

Feet on the Ground
and Human Resources

Who Runs the Show?

Thinking of running a business abroad? If you
employ local people, you're naturally the boss.
But the local government regulates your
operations. So who runs the show?

WHEN I WAS A YOUNG, ONLY CHILD, and my father told me to do something, we would always have this exchange:

Me: Why do I have to do that?
Dad: Because I'm the boss.
Me: Well, then who am I the boss of?
Dad: You're the boss of the bugs.

It's sort of a silly little exchange between a father and child, but it reminds me a lot of running a business abroad. As a business's leader, you play the father role to the local employees, but you also play also the child role to the host-nation's government.

For the sake of this section, we'll assume you plan on operating the business you incorporated in your home country, but also now are starting to operate on another country's soil. Some countries will not allow this because of a desire to protect domestic businesses and prevent the tax losses, but many countries do. There are pros and cons to both, which I'll talk a bit about later.

Different profiles for businesses in host nations

Here's the thing about running a business overseas: Countries are as unique and different as can be when it comes to foreign business regulations, work permits, labor laws, governmental involvement in your business, taxes, etc. The best way to learn the ins and outs of who runs the show, as it pertains to you, is to examine the rules of the target country. You may well want to hire a local attorney to help with this.

In general, as long as you're running your business within the host-nation's rules and regulations, you are free to run your operation as you see fit. Host countries will typically be more welcoming to companies who come in and hire a lot of local people than to, say, a self-employed graphic designer from Canada who wants to live and work in his Paris apartment, but plans to maintain his Canadian citizenship, pay Canadian income taxes, and not employ any French citizens in his business. The French government may not deny the Canadian graphic designer his work permit, but it would a lot happier if he grew his business, purchased or rented a large office space in Paris, and employed 15 French graphic designers.

As you've seen from all the foregoing sections, before you make the decision to open an office, shop or factory or move your entire business overseas, you really need to do your homework on costs, feasibility, local government regulations, taxes, etc. While it may truly be financially beneficial, more companies go bankrupt trying to move their operation overseas than any other reason, mostly due to inadequate planning.

Plan and test

I'm not trying to dissuade you. More than anything, I want you to be happy doing business, wherever you end up. I just don't want to see you fall into the trap that has swallowed up so many others. When you're conducting your research on the host nation or area, ensure you do a full market test of the area, just as you would if you were starting a small business if your home town.

It's harder conducting a market test abroad, especially if the laws differ a lot from your home country's, and *especially* if the language is different and you're not at least conversational. Think about this, too; have you begun paperwork for renting or purchasing the space you will need? What language is it in? Have you had your home country's attorney look at it? Do you need a local attorney? All the same rules apply for starting or moving your business overseas as if you were moving it to another part of your home country. The only difference is that there are a multitude of variables that can be easily overlooked which can be crippling and/or costly if you find them out too late. And some mistakes can even hurt you back in your home market. For example, Nike suffered significant bad publicity when the working conditions in their overseas factories made the news in the US.

Buying a local business

Because it can be difficult and risky it to start a business from scratch abroad, purchasing an already established local business there may be more likely the way to go… for a few reasons. For starters, the business is already up and running, and may even already have local employees (who you would be smart to keep, at least for the time being). Additionally, there is likely already a clientele in place, local folks who should wander in on Day One, expecting the same service as always.

As in your home country, however, it's essential to do some research to learn *why* the business is for sale in the first place. There are firms that specialize in transitioning business owners, and from your home country, they can connect with their folks in or near the country you desire to relocate or expand into, in order to conduct a business evaluation, market test, account audit, etc. This will alleviate a lot of the risk and probably save you time and money down the road. With or without such advisors, take the time to understand every page of documentation you intend to sign, inside and out.

   Previously, we discussed the pros and cons to owning a company in a foreign country vs. having to conduct all business through a local intermediary. Consider the automotive industry. In many countries, there are domestic as well as foreign car companies, all competing for customers. Whatever country the car company is incorporated in is the country that collects the income taxes on that company's revenue, which would be considered a win for that country. However, if a foreign car company comes to a new country, builds a huge car manufacturing plant and employs and pays 5,000 local citizens to work in the plant building cars, then the host country will get to collect the income taxes from the 5,000 local employees. So you can see how I said there were pros and cons to each.

S.G. and M.R.M.

Managing at a Distance

*Distance can be physical or cultural, or both. It pays
to be conscious of the impact of distance
when you manage across borders.*

AMONG THE MANY FASCINATING CHALLENGES you may face when doing international business is how you manage others who are somewhere else, perhaps someplace very different from where you are. A little forethought can prevent expensive missteps and save money, while getting the most from the people you work with.

Let's suppose you've gotten up to speed with the culture (if not the language) of the people you manage long-distance, whether via reading, visiting or living for a while in the target market. You may have local people working for you. Or perhaps you've dispatched an employee to work abroad. The tips below will make your task easier and reduce the static that can sabotage communications, damage good will, and harm results. Some tips contradict others, but you can judge which action is best in a given situation. The tips fall into several broad categories.

Leadership

Build trust. Major global consulting firms like the Center for Creative Leadership report that trust, change and collaboration are the top leadership challenges these days. If you can build trust with the people you lead and manage, it opens the way to solving almost any internal issue despite distance and differences.

Find good people. It's well known that if you manage a person who just isn't right for the job, you can do everything right and still not get the results you want. So when you engage or hire someone abroad, or select someone from home to go live there, do all you can to get the right person from the start. Check references, do trial projects, role play, agree on a trial work period, specify targets and milestones that are measurable. Make time periodically to discuss and evaluate performance, and if it's not going right, take steps quickly to change the situation (be sure you know the implications if you need to replace the person) and move on. Review the job description for its feasibility before rehiring.

Focus on goals. It's your job to ensure that those you manage really know what they are to do and how their work contributes to the larger picture. At a distance, goals can become fuzzy very quickly, and you end up with a Lone Ranger or even a Rebel who's got a totally different picture of what the goal is.

Be systematic. As much as possible, try to limit the randomness of your business activity. Your employees appreciate knowing how you operate and what you expect. They have enough challenges adapting to your strange ways too.

Assert. Notice this is not a suggestion that you be stubborn, aggressive, rude or bully people. You are the manager, however, and you need to lead with confidence and clarity, however unsure you may feel about the challenges that distances bring. It's fine to assert, but also to admit mistakes or misunderstandings and to fix them. Particularly if your intuitions tell you something isn't right, use your position to shine light on things and respond correctly.

Recognize cultural differences in manager-employee relations. Your employee abroad may be meek, brash, passive, rebellious, overly complimentary or deferential, or otherwise treat you in culturally defined ways. In some cultures, you must take into account the need to save face, or to overcome traditional prejudices or practices. You need to separate personal from cultural styles and work with them as you find them.

Communication

Share an agenda. A lot of managers just order tasks to be done. It works better to follow the PPP pattern in your communications so everybody shares the agenda from the start, at home and abroad.

PPP stands for Purpose-Process-Payoff. At the start of a meeting, phone call or email, explicitly tell people abroad why you are taking time for this event, how you plan to go through it, and what the benefit or goal—the payoff—will be. This can be done in less than a minute. Here are some examples:

- "For the next 30 minutes I'd like to review your August sales figures (Purpose). Let's start with the Northern region and then discuss the South (Process). That way we can quickly review the North's growth and focus most of our time on the problems the South is facing (Payoff). Is that okay with you?"

- "Hi Charlie, it's Pat. I'm calling to confirm that our delivery will be late after all, and to decide with you which way is best to ship (Purpose). Let's review our options and make a final choice of transporters, via air or rail (Process). That way our logistics team can get quotes on air vs. rail delivery, and we will know what the final cost will be (Payoff). Okay?

- "This email is to summarize the steps we routinely take to hire a new worker (Purpose). You will find attached all the documents you need to fill out, with comments in red. Please review them and reply with your comments and questions by March 14th, 09.00 Eastern US time (Process). This will help us gear up for the big order of widgets we need to deliver by January 1st (Payoff). I look forward to your input."

You'll notice that in addition to the PPP structure, each example ends in a kind of agreement or commitment action. That's important, because the other person may well have problems or questions about what you're proposing to do. Those need to be addressed before you begin the process.*

Document. After a meeting or important phone call, jot down and share your summary of the key points and actions, with deadlines and who does what. Over a distance, these things can fall out of focus. Your document will serve as a reminder and a measuring stick of progress.

Play back. Similarly, if you run into either differences of opinion or lack of clarity, it's good to play back the final agreed version of the truth. "So just to be sure we all agree, the deadline is the last day of the month, whether it's a work day or not. Right?"

Attitude

Be patient. Managing at a distance is trying for both sides. Try to adapt your expectations of what can be done to the real situation and allow for the inevitable disconnects and mistakes that seem much more annoying when you can't walk down the hall to settle something.

Go slow. Of course, you can't always do this. But slow and steady does deliver pretty well over distant team activities. Balance this approach with the moments when a sense of urgency is what really is needed. And be aware that the pace of business really varies a lot around the world.

Empathize. Being able to put yourself in another's shoes goes a long way to being a good manager, anywhere. At a distance, it can be very frustrating for both parties if they are coping with the typical challenges of global business, like time zones and language gaps—and the reality that they were up all night with a

---

*You can learn more about Purpose-Process-Payoff techniques in the Wilson Learning Library book, *Win-Win Selling* (Nova Vista Publishing, ISBN 978-90-77256-34-3). It is available in both print and e-book formats.

sick child, or the electricity cut off again during a key process, or the bank is closed for a national holiday you forgot about.

Be cautious, even skeptical. Unfortunately, it at a distance it can be hard to tell if you're being bamboozled. In small and large matters, distance can be used as a cover for mischief or worse. Be creative about finding ways to double-check things. Too many international managers take reports, numbers, commitments and even threats at face value, and the consequences can be serious.

Probe. If you suspect something is wrong, be creative about probing. Do you need to make an unscheduled visit or have a trusted local third party test the validity of what you are being told? (And by the way, this point does not assume you are dealing with a local national. Your own expat employee on assignment abroad could be just as vulnerable to temptations or mistakes.)

Surround. Do some creative thinking about checks and balances, information loops, sign-offs, etc. These don't have to be embarrassing to the people you manage if you can present them as the way you routinely work.

Language

Repeat. It's not insulting to restate key points, perhaps by summarizing them or giving an example. Sometimes, where language is an issue, this can help clarify a point that the other person doesn't get, without having to call attention to the language gap.

Don't get fancy. When language is an issue, try hard to use the simplest language you can, and cut out any unnecessary content. Don't use metaphors based on your culture or which have a hidden meaning, like "Bob's your uncle." "I've got your back." "Madder than a wet hen." "Give a dog and pony show." "Way off base." Such phrases fog up rather than directly say what you mean, and lead to confusion and wasted time.

Don't bluff. If it's *your* language skill that's in question, don't pretend to understand things you don't. It may be embarrassing to stop the conversation, but usually it's better to get the point correctly than to miss it.

Tools

Take small steps. If necessary, break tasks or processes into smaller bits and supply lots of job aids, feedback loops, etc. to keep things on track.

Use technology. As much as you can, make use of the technologies that allow you to see, share and interact live over the distance. We all know how tone and body language tell volumes, and that goes for giving encouragement, correction, and a wealth of other kinds of messages—and also for picking up clues from the other person as well.

Humor. Carefully and sensitively applied, humor can be a wonderful bridge across all kinds of barriers. Consider it as a powerful management tool.

In the end, building solid, trusting relationships with those you manage at a distance is a challenge that has great rewards when it works right. It's worth investing time, thought and energy in this aspect of your global business, because it's actually part of the foundation and a key to success.

K.S.

Afterword:
Where to Go from Here?

IT MAY BE SAFE TO ASSUME that if you've just finished reading this book, you are one of two types of individuals. The *curious* reader may have been interested in learning how a potentially successful business could be envisioned, created and then finally launched to compete in a foreign market. For curious readers, these pages may have even sparked your imagination about becoming an international entrepreneur one day.

The *serious* reader may have chosen to read our book because he or she may have already decided to become a global entrepreneur. Or perhaps, you've launched your business, and now additional tools, expert guidance, and real-world examples of international business issues are vital to your success.

Curious or serious, we hope that everyone who has read this sixth volume of our series found the material worthy of your time. Regardless of how or why you found us, we are glad you did.

For the three of us who founded the Expert Business Advice website, and for Mark Moon in his legal practice, and Kate Scribner in her international business, the philosophy is simple:

- Create material of substance and value that can continue to be expanded indefinitely for the benefit of the reader, the customer, and the business professional
- Deliver the best possible ideas, resources and guidance to those who seek it
- Take ownership of our work, stand by it, and be proud of it

Developing this material from several points of view and delivering it to people from diverse backgrounds and with multiple levels of experience was crucial for us. In fact, it was the only way we could imagine doing it.

Simply put, our goal with this series shares the same vision as Expert Business Advice's slogan: "Experts Create | We Deliver | You Apply."

The way forward begins here…

Acknowledgements

WE HAVE A LOT OF THANKS TO GIVE.

Scott Girard wishes to thank his wife Kellin, his co-authors, his parents, the Girard Family, the Conway Family, the Edwards Family, the Seaman Family, the Warren Family (keep up the writing, Lea), the O'Keefe Family, the Thomas Family, the Price Family, everyone at Pinpoint Holdings Group, Barbara Stephens, Jack Chambless, Mary-Jo Tracy, Sandra McMonagle, Diane Orsini, Nathan Holic, Peter Telep, Pat Rushin, and the Seminole Battalion.

Mike O'Keefe wishes to thank his parents Tim and Gaye O'Keefe, his co-authors, Jamie, Kimberly Rupert, the O'Keefe Family, the Goldsberry Family, the Roy Family, the Hubert Family, the Murat Family, the Grant Family, the Girard Family, the Price Family, the Holycross Family, the most inspiring professor Jack Chambless, his two favorite authors Clive Cussler and Timothy Ferriss, and those individuals in Argentina (for making sure there is always Malbec on the table).

Marc Price wishes to thank his wife Dawn; his co-authors; his mom Lynda; the Price Family; the O'Bryan Family; the Smith Family; Jean Hughes; the O'Keefe Family; the Girard Family; Mike Schiano; David Wittschen and Family; Kurt Ardaman; Axum Coffee in Winter Garden, Florida; and his life-long mentor, Howard Satin.

Mark Moon wishes to thank his wife, Marguerite, for sticking with him and for being his pillar of strength; he will always love her, truly, madly and deeply. He would like to thank their entire family for being so understanding of everything he does. He would like to thank his professional mentors for making him the practitioner he is today, especially Paul Tabio, Lee-Ford Tritt, Dennis A. Calfee, Richard Gallant, Vaughn Brown, Julio Acosta, Eugene Meisenheimer, Paul McGarr and Anne Nymark. Mark would like to thank the Moon Law Group team who make the dream work every day: Donna Casavant, Rhonda Orlosky, Melissa McCoy, Katrina Spriet, Mary Huntsman, Mai Vu and Mark Sodhi. He would like to thank his peers, who continue to inspire and drive him: Brian McKenzie, Adam Sudbury, Josh Law, Ingrid Hooglander, Joryn Jenkins, Brad Goodwin, Jasen Pask, Josh Walker, Scott Girard, Matthew Tebow, Justin Egan and Tad Schnaufer. Finally, Mark would like to thank all of his past, present and future clients for providing him the opportunity to do what he loves to do on a daily basis.

Kate Scribner wishes to thank Jo Dupré, Cy DeCosse, Jim Maus, Wilson Learning Worldwide, Lynn Collins, and the many other international business colleagues who have taught, supported, challenged and shared the fun of international business with her over the years.

The authors would collectively like to thank Kathe Grooms and everyone at Nova Vista Publishing, everyone at Expert Business Advice, Jon Collier, and the Van Beekum Family: Dave, Melissa and the Sugar Gliders.

Glossary

Accountant One who is trained and qualified in the practice of accounting or who is in charge of public or private accounts.

Accounting The systematic recording, reporting and analysis of the financial transactions of a business or government.

Accredited Investor A term defined by various countries' securities laws that characterizes investors permitted to invest in certain types of higher risk investments including seed money, limited partnerships, hedge funds, private placements, and angel investor networks. The term generally includes wealthy individuals and financially-oriented organizations such as banks, insurance companies, significant charities, some corporations, endowments, and retirement plans.

Advertising A form of communication used to encourage or motivate an audience to take or continue to take some new action. Most commonly, the desired result is to guide consumer behavior regarding a commercial offering.

Agent Someone with expressed or implied authority to act for another person or business (the principal) to bring the principal into contractual relationships with other parties., e.g., a sales agent, purchasing agent.

Alibaba Currently the world's largest online commerce company; headquartered in China.

Angel Investor An individual who provides funding to one or more start-up companies. The individual is usually affluent or has a personal interest in the success of the venture. Such investments are distinguished by high levels of risk and a potentially large return on investment.

Asylum Seekers People who leave their own country, often for political reasons, and travel to another country, hoping that the government will protect and allow them to live there.

B2B	See *Business to Business*.
Balance Sheet	A quantitative synopsis of a company's financial condition at a specific point in time, including assets, liabilities and net worth. The first part of a balance sheet illustrates all the productive assets a company owns, and the second part shows all the financing methods (such as liabilities and shareholders' equity). Also called a statement of condition.
Bi-Lateral Netting	Settlement of mutual obligations between two parties where the net difference (not the gross amounts) is carried forward; common practice in trading of foreign exchange, futures, and options.
Black Money	Unaccounted-for and untaxed cash generated by dealings in a black economy, black market, or organized crime. Holders of black money typically try to convert it into legitimate money through money laundering.
Blog	A personal journal published on the Internet consisting of discrete entries, called *posts*, typically displayed in reverse chronological order so the most recent post appears first.
Board of Directors	Individuals elected by a business's shareholders to oversee the management of the business.
Bookkeeping	The systematic transcription of a business's financial transactions.
Bottom Line	The amount left after taxes, interest, depreciation, and other expenses are subtracted from gross sales. Also called net earnings, net income, or net profit.
Brainstorming	A group creativity technique in which members spontaneously and freely generate a list of ideas to address a specific opportunity or problem.
Brain-Trust Equity	Equity that is accepted or earned through an individual's contribution of information, ideas, or concepts to the strategic growth, development or direction of a company and its products, services or organizational structure.
Brand	An identifying symbol, word, phrase or mark that identifies and distinguishes a product or business from its competitors.

Branding

The act of identifying a product or business and distinguishing it from its competitors by utilizing unique symbols, words, or marks.

Bribery

The act of taking or receiving something of value with the intention of influencing the recipient in some way favorable to the party providing the bribe.

Brick-and-Mortar Business

A description of a company or portion of a company with a physical presence, as opposed to one that exists only virtually, on the Internet.

Budget

An itemized prediction of an individual's or business's income and expenses expected for some period in the future.

Budget Deficit

The amount by which a business or individual's spending exceeds its income over a specific period of time.

Business

A commercial activity engaged in as a means of occupation or income, or an entity which engages in such activities.

Business Consultant

An individual or company that provides advising, analyzing, monitoring, training, reviewing or reporting services to commercial clients.

Business License

Permits issued by government agencies that grant individuals or companies the right to conduct business within the government's geographical jurisdiction. It is the authorization to start a new business issued by the local government.

Business Model

A description of the operations of a business including the segments of the business; its functions, roles and relationships; and the revenues and expenses that the business generates.

Business Operations

Ongoing recurring activities involved in running a business in order to generate value for its stakeholders.

Business Plan

A document prepared by a company's management, or by a consultant on their behalf, that details the past, present, and future of the company, usually for the purpose of attracting capital investment.

Business Taxes

Taxes owed and paid by a corporate entity.

Business to Business   Trading between firms, characterized by relatively large volumes, competitive and stable prices, fast delivery times and, often, on a deferred payment basis. In general, wholesaling.

Buyout   The purchase or acquisition of controlling interest in one corporation by another corporation, in order to take over assets and/or operations.

C-Corporation   A business which, unlike a partnership, is a completely separate entity from its owners. Also called a C-Corp.

Capital   1. Cash or goods used to produce income either by investing in a business or a different income property.

2. The net worth of a company; that is, the amount by which its assets exceed its liabilities.

3. The money, property, and other valuables which collectively represent the value of an individual or business.

Capital Expenditure   Money spent to acquire or enhance physical assets such as buildings and machinery. Also called capital spending or capital expense.

Capital Requirements   The amount of cash a business needs for its normal operations.

Cash Capital Disbursement   The repaying of a debt or expense.

Cash Flow Positive   The situation when income exceeds liabilities.

Cash Flow Statement   A summary of a business's cash flow over a given period of time.

Chat Room   Any form of online communication in which participants type and send their thoughts, taking turns sequentially, as in chatting, either in real time or asynchronously. Useful for electronic instant communication among several people.

Collateral   Assets pledged by a borrower to secure a loan or other credit, and subject to seizure in the event of default. Also called security.

Company Description   The third section of a business plan. A brief synopsis that describes how all of the different components in a business work together.

Competitor	A business or person that provides similar products or services.
Consultant	Experienced professional who provides expert knowledge for a fee.
Contingency Plan	A plan devised for an outcome other than the one in the expected plan.
Contract	A binding agreement between two or more parties for taking action, or refraining from taking action, sometimes in exchange for lawful monetary or other consideration.
Controlling Interest	The ownership of a majority of a company's voting stock; or a significant fraction, even if less than the majority, if the rest of the shares are not actively voted.
Conversion Rate	In commerce, the rate at which a commodity, currency, or a type of security can be exchanged for another.
Convertible Debt	Security which can be converted for a specified amount of another, related security, at the option of the issuer and/or the holder. Also called convertible.
Copyright	The exclusive right to produce and dispose of copies of a literary, musical, or artistic work.
Corp.	The abbreviation for *corporation*.
Corporation	The most common form of business organization, which is given many legal rights as an entity separate from its owners. This form of business is characterized by the limited liability of its owners, the issuance of shares of easily transferable stock, and existence as a going concern.
Credentials	A tangible representation of qualification, competence, or authority issued to an individual by a third party with a relevant authority or assumed competence to do so.
Credit	The borrowing ability of an individual or company.
Credit History	A record of an individual's or company's past borrowing and repaying behavior.
Credit Report	A report comprised of detailed information on a person's credit history.

Credit Score	A numerically represented measure of credit risk calculated from a credit report using a standardized formula.
Creditworthiness	A creditor's measure of an individual's or company's ability to meet debt responsibilities.
Currency Fluctuations	The continual adjustment of the relative values of two currencies, as a result of the floating currency exchange rate system that most major economies use.
Curriculum Vitae	A résumé; an overview of a person's experience and other qualifications. Also called a CV.
Customer Service	The supply of service to customers before, during and after a purchase.
Database	An organized accumulation of data, today typically in digital form. The data are typically organized to depict relevant aspects of reality, in a way that supports processes requiring this information.
Debt	An amount owed to a person or organization for funds borrowed.
Debt Financing	Financing by selling bonds, bills or notes to individuals or businesses.
Debt Retirement	The repayment of a debt.
Debt-to-Income Ratio	A figure that calculates how much income is spent repaying debts.
Deduction	An expense subtracted from adjusted gross income when calculating taxable income. Also called tax deduction.
Demographics	Data on socioeconomic groups, e.g., age, income, sex, education, occupation, etc., often used to study or profile a target market.
Design Patent	A patent issued on the ornamental design of a functional item.
Disclaimer	A statement made to remove oneself from responsibility. Also called hedge clause.
Dividend	A taxable cash award declared by a company's board of directors and given to its shareholders out of the company's current or retained earnings, usually quarterly. Also used as a slang term to mean reward.

Domain Name	An identification string (sequence of letters and perhaps numbers) that defines a realm of administrative autonomy, authority, or control on the world wide web. For example, www.expertbusinessadvice.com.
Double Taxation	Taxation of the same income by two governments, or of income at two levels (e.g., taxation of income at both the personal and corporate level).
e-Commerce	The buying and selling of products and services by businesses and consumers through an electronic medium, without using any paper documents.
Economics	The study of how the forces of supply and demand assign scarce resources.
Economy	Activities related to the production and distribution of goods and services in a specific geographic region.
Elevator Speech	A very concise presentation of a concept or business model covering all of its critical aspects, able to be delivered within a few seconds (the approximate duration of an elevator ride). Also called an elevator pitch.
Emigration	The act of leaving a home country or place of residence to live elsewhere.
Eminent Domain	Legal doctrine of the right and inherent power of a government to take private property for public use upon reimbursing the owner with the fair market value of the property.
Entrepreneur	An individual who starts his or her own business.
EPO	Acronym for European Patent Office.
Equity	Ownership interest in a business in the form of common stock or preferred stock.
Equity Financing	Financing a business by selling common or preferred stock to investors.
European Patent Office	One of the two offices of the European Patent Organization. The other is the Administrative Council.
Exchange Rates	Price for which the currency of a country can be exchanged for another country's currency.

Executive Summary   The first section of a business plan. A synopsis of the entire plan, along with a brief history of the company.

Expense   Any cost of conducting business.

Expense Report   A document that contains all the expenses that a business has incurred as a result of the business's operation.

Expropriation   Compulsory seizure or surrender of private property for the state's purposes, with little or no compensation to the property's owner (also can be nationalization).

Farming Out   A slang term for outsourcing, in which organizations hire vendors to perform duties the organizations choose not to do themselves in-house.

Financial Adviser   A person or organization employed by a business or mutual fund to manage assets or provide investment advice.

Financials   Documents related to finance.

Financing   Providing the necessary monetary capital.

Fixed Expense   An expense that does not change depending on production or sales levels, such as rent, property tax, insurance, or interest expense. Also called fixed cost.

Flow Chart   A formalized graphic representation of a work or manufacturing process.

Franchise   A form of business organization in which a company which already has a successful product or service (the franchisor) enters into a continuing contractual agreement with other businesses (franchisees) operating under the franchisor's trade name, usually with the franchisor's guidance, in exchange for a fee.

Franchising   The practice of licensing a successful business model.

Fulfillment   Accomplishment. Also can mean storing, order processing and shipment of goods.

General Partner   A partner with unlimited legal obligation for the debts and liabilities of a partnership.

Grant   Funds disbursed by the grantor to a recipient.

Graphic Design   A method of artistic marketing used to create and combine words, symbols, and images to create a visual representation of ideas and messages.

Gross Margin	A measure of profitability, often shortened to GM. To calculate divide Gross Income by Net Sales, and express it as a percentage. For example, a widget sells for $5 and costs $3 to make.
	$5 (Net Sales) - $3 (Cost of Goods) = $2 (Gross Income).
	Then 2 ÷ 5 = 0.4, which expressed as a percentage is 40% Gross Margin.
Growth Rate	A measure of financial growth.
Growth Strategy	A plan of action based on investing in companies and sectors which are growing faster than their peers. Also can mean an organization's plan for increasing, expanding, and otherwise getting bigger.
Hardware	A general term for equipment that can be touched. In business, *hardware* most commonly refers to computer hardware; laptops, desktops, monitors, etc. In general, computer software operates on computer hardware.
Home-Based Business	A small business that operates from the business owner's home. Also called a home business.
Hyperlink	A reference to data that the operator can directly follow, or that is followed automatically. A hyperlink points to an entire document or to a specific element within a document.
Immigration	The action of moving across borders to live permanently in a foreign country.
Inc.	Abbreviation for incorporated.
Income	Revenues minus cost of sales, operating expenses, and taxes, over a given period of time.
Income Statement	A document illustrating sales, expenses, and net profit for a given period.
Incorporated	A business that has been formed into a legal corporation by completing the required procedures.
Indemnity Bond	An insurance bond used as an additional measure of security to cover loan amounts, worth about 75 percent of the value of the property. This bond protects lenders from loss, in the event that the borrower defaults on the loan.

Industry Standard

A practice accepted as convention by industry members, either through formal agreement or through emulation of best practices established by industry leaders.

Infrastructure

Relatively permanent and foundational capital investment of a country, firm, or project that underlies and makes possible all its economic activity. Examples: road or rail systems, communication or electrical grids.

INGO

Acronym for International Intergovernmental Organizations.

Initial Public Offering

The initial sale of stock by a company to the public.

Intellectual Property

Any intangible asset that is comprised of human knowledge and ideas.

Interest

The return earned on an investment.

Internal Revenue Service

The federal agency of the United States responsible for administering and enforcing the US Treasury Department's revenue laws, through the assessment and collection of taxes, determination of pension plan qualification, and related activities.

International Intergovernmental Organization

An organization composed primarily of soveriegn states (referred to as member states), or of intergovernmental organizations.

Internet

Commonly called a network of networks, the Internet is a global system of interconnected computer networks that use the standard Internet protocol suite to serve billions of users worldwide.

Internet Marketing

The marketing of products or services over the Internet. Also called web marketing, online marketing, webvertising, and e-marketing.

Internship

On-the-job training for college (or sometimes high school) students.

Interview

A discussion between two people where questions are asked by the interviewer in order to gather information from the interviewee. Often part of a hiring process.

Investment Banker

An individual who acts as an underwriter or agent for businesses and municipalities issuing securities.

Investment Group	A group of investors who pool some of their money and make joint investments. Also called an investment club.
Investor	An individual who commits monetary capital to investment products with the expectation of financial return.
IP Address	Internet Protocol Address. A numerical identification assigned to each device participating in a computer network that uses the Internet Protocol for communication.
IPO	Acronym for Initial Public Offering.
Keyword	A word or identifier that has a specific meaning to the programming language.
Legal Representation	An attorney, lawyer, barrister or solicitor.
Lending Portfolio	A collection of investments all owned by the same person or organization.
Letter of Reference	A letter in which an employer, past or present, recommends someone for a new job. Also called a letter of recommendation.
Leveraged Buyout	The takeover of a company or controlling interest of a company (a buyout), involving a significant amount of borrowed (leveraged) money.
Liability	An obligation that legally commits an individual or company to settle a debt.
Licensing	Under defined conditions, the granting of permission to use intellectual property rights, such as trademarks, patents, or technology.
Limited Liability Company	A type of company, authorized only in certain business sectors, whose owners and managers receive the limited liability and tax benefits of an S-Corporation without having to conform to S-Corporation restrictions.
Limited Partner	In a corporate entity with one or more general partners, limited partners are liable only to the extent of their investments. Limited partners also enjoy rights to the partnership's cash flow, but are not liable for company obligations.
Links	See *hyperlinks*.

Liquidation	The process of converting assets or investments into cash.
Liquidity	The ability of an asset or property to be converted into cash quickly and without any price discount.
LLC	Acronym for limited liability company.
Loan	An arrangement in which a lender gives monetary capital or property to a borrower, and the borrower agrees to return the property or repay the monetary capital, usually along with interest, at some future point in time.
Logo	A graphic mark or wordmark used by individuals or organizations to aid and promote instant public recognition.
Mandate	A command or order.
Margin	See *Gross Margin*.
Market Analysis	Research intended to predict the expectations of a market.
Marketing	The process by which products and services are announced and launched into the marketplace.
Marketing Plan	A written document that illustrates the necessary actions to achieve one or more marketing objectives. It can be for a product or service, a brand, or a product line.
Marketplace	The area—actual, virtual or metaphorical—in which a market operates.
Market Penetration	Occurs when a business penetrates a market in which products or services already exist.
Market Segment	A collection of consumers that share multiple characteristics (e.g., demographics, behavior, psychographic similarities, geographic relationships with unmet or underserved needs) that is large and accessible enough to present a reasonable marketing opportunity for a business.
Market Share	The percentage of the total sales of a given type of product or service that is won by given company.
Market Test	A geographic region or demographic group used to gauge the applicability of a product or service in a marketplace, prior to a wide-scale launch.

Media	Entities used to store and deliver information or data.
Merchant Banking	An investment bank which is well-equipped to manage multinational corporations. Commonly, electronic.
Middleman	Intermediary between two commercial entities, commonly a wholesaler or distributor who buys from a manufacturer and sells to a retailer or to consumer.
Mission Statement	A mission statement is a statement of the purpose of a business or organization.
Multimedia	Combined use of multiple media.
Municipality	An administrative division that has corporate status and usually self-governing powers.
Nationalization	Takeover of privately owned corporations, industries, and resources by a government, with or without compensation.
NDA	Acronym for non-disclosure agreement.
Network	An arrangement of connections.
Non-Disclosure Agreement	A contract that prohibits the disclosure of confidential information or proprietary knowledge under specific circumstances.
Open Market	A market which is widely and generally accessible to all investors or consumers.
Operating Expense	An expense arising in the normal course of running a business, such as manufacturing, advertising and sales.
OPEX	Acronym for operating expense.
Outsourcing	Work executed for a business by people other than the business's full-time employees.
Over-Saturated Market	In a market occupied by buyers and sellers, a market that is filled with sellers to the point that it negatively affects each seller's opportunity to make a significant profit. Also called a saturated market.
Owner-Operated	An organization that is operated in full or in majority by its owner.
Ownership Equity	The owner's share of the assets of a business.
Partners	Members of a partnership, either general or limited.

Partnership
A relationship of two or more entities, people or companies, conducting business for mutual benefit.

Passion
Intense emotion; used in business to identify positive dedication and engagement by someone with an idea, activity, role, etc.

Patent
The exclusive right, granted by the government, to use an invention or process for a given period of time, usually 14 years.

Patent Law Treaty
A multilateral patent law treaty concluded on 1 June 2000 in Geneva, Switzerland by 53 States and the European Patent Organization, with the aim of regularizing or coordinating formal procedures such as the requirements to obtain a filing date for a patent application, the form and content of a patent application, and representation.

Payment Bond
A surety bond through which a contractor assures an owner that material and labor provided in the completion of a project will be fully paid for, and that no mechanics' liens will be filed against the owner.

Performance Bond
A bond issued to guarantee adequate and acceptable completion of a project by a contractor.

Permit
The legal authorization or physical item which grants someone permission to do something.

Personal Finances
One's private funds, property, possessions. The application of finance principles to the monetary decisions of a person or family.

Piracy
In business, the unauthorized reproduction of an intellectual property in infringement of copyright law. Can also be the manufacturing of "fake" goods bearing well-known brands, or unauthorized copies of compact disks and the like.

Press Release
A written or recorded message directed at members of the news media and others of potential interest for the purpose of announcing something newsworthy. Also called a news release, media release, or press statement.

Price Point
A point on a range of possible prices at which something might be marketed.

Principle
A rule or ethical standard.

Private Labeling	A retailer's name, as used on a product sold by the retailer but manufactured by another company.
Private Placement	The sale of shares directly to an institutional investor, such as a bank, mutual fund, insurance company, pension fund, or foundation.
Pro Forma	Description of financial statements that have one or more assumptions or hypothetical conditions built into the data. Often used with balance sheets and income statements when data is not available, to construct scenarios. One variety is called a Pro Forma Income Statement. Another is a Pro Forma Invoice.
Profit	The positive gain from an investment or business operation after deducting all expenses.
Project Timeline	The internally allocated time frame of a project from start to finish.
Promissory Note	A document signed by a borrower promising to repay a loan under agreed-upon terms. Also called a note.
Proof of Concept	Evidence from a market test or trial period that demonstrates that a business model or idea is feasible.
Publicity	Information that attracts attention to a business, product, person, or event.
Qualitative Research	A method of inquiry designed to reveal a target audience's range of behavior and the perceptions that drive it with reference to specific topics or issues.
Quantitative Research	A method of inquiry designed to reveal social phenomena via statistical, mathematical or numerical data or computational techniques.
Quota	In trade, a limitation placed by governments on the amount of goods or services offered for sale within the government's jurisdiction by organizations based outside that area.
R&D	Acronym for Research and Development.
Research	The process of acquiring and organizing information for the purpose of initiating, modifying or terminating a particular investment or group of investments.

Research and Development	Acquiring new knowledge about products, processes, and services, and then applying that knowledge to create new and improved products, processes, and services that fill the needs of the market.
Résumé	A brief written synopsis of an individual's education, work experience, and accomplishments, typically for the purposes of finding a job. Also called a curriculum vitae, or CV.
Revenue	The total amount of money received by an organization for goods or services provided during a certain time period. Sometimes called turnover.
Reverse Privatization	See *Nationalization*.
Risk	The quantifiable probability of loss or less-than-expected returns.
RSS Feed	Acronym for RDF Site Summary (although most commonly dubbed "Really Simple Syndication"). A congregation of web feed formats used to publish and automatically syndicate frequently updated works, such as blog entries, news headlines, audio, and video, in a standardized format.
S-Corporation	A type of corporation, recognized in the US by the Internal Revenue Service for most companies with 75 or fewer shareholders, which enables the company to enjoy the benefits of incorporation but be taxed as if it were a partnership. Also called Subchapter S Corporation, or S-Corp.
Sales	Total monetary amount collected for goods and services provided.
Sales Activity	The act of selling.
Sales Force	A group of people whose only corporate responsibility is to sell a company's products or services.
Sales Force Strategy	The strategic plan of a sales force to penetrate and have lasting impact on the market.
Sanction	Formal approval or authorization; in trade, usually used to mean a limitation of the activity permitted by governments on traders as a way of influencing other countries' policies or actions.

SBA

Acronym for the Small Business Administration in the US.

SBA Loan

A business loan issued by the US Small Business Administration.

Search Engine

Designed to search for information on the World Wide Web, search engines generally produce results presented in a list, often referred to as search engine results pages (SERPs). The information may consist of web pages, images, information and other types of files.

Search Engine Optimization

The process of improving the popularity of a website or a web page in search engines' un-paid ("natural") search results. In general, the earlier (or higher ranked on the search results page), and more frequently a site appears in the search results list, the more visitors it will receive from the search engine's users.

SEO

Acronym for search engine optimization.

Server

A physical computer hardware system dedicated to running one or more services, as a host, to serve the needs of users of the other computers on the network.

Shareholder

One who owns shares of stock in a corporation or mutual fund. For corporations, along with the ownership comes a right to declared dividends and the right to vote on certain company matters, including the board of directors. Also called a stockholder.

Site Traffic

The amount and flow of visitors to a website.

Small Business Administration

A US Federal agency which offers loans to small businesses.

Social Media

Web-based and mobile technologies used to turn communication into interactive dialogue between organizations, communities, and individuals. They are ubiquitously accessible, and enabled by scalable communication techniques.

Socioeconomics

Referring to social and economic conditions, social classes and income groups.

Software

A accumulation of computer programs and related data that provides the instructions that tell a computer what to do and how to do it.

Sole Proprietorship	A company which is not registered with the state as a limited liability company or corporation and is a business structure in which an individual and his/her company are considered a single entity for tax and liability purposes.
Stakeholder	Anyone who is interested in or affected by something; one who could benefit from information about it. Not to be confused with shareholders.
Start-up	1. The beginning of a new company or new product. 2. A new, usually small business that is just beginning its operations, especially a new business supported by venture capital and in a sector where new technologies are used.
Start-Up Capital	The initial stage in financing a new project, which is followed by several rounds of investment capital as the project gets under way
Statement of Cash Flows	A summary of a company's cash flow over a given period of time. Also called Cash Flow Statement.
Stock Symbol	Ticker symbol for a stock.
Strategy	A planned system of action.
Strengths	Actions a business accomplishes exceptionally or easily; assets.
Subsidy	Financial aid given by the government to individuals or groups.
Surety Bond	A bond issued by an entity on behalf of a second party, guaranteeing that the second party will fulfill an obligation or series of obligations to a third party. In the event that the obligations are not met, the third party can recover its losses via the bond.
SWOT Analysis	An assessment of an organization's strengths, weaknesses, opportunities and threats.
Synopsis	A summary.
Takeover	Acquiring control of a corporation, called a target, by stock purchase or exchange, either hostile or friendly.
Target Market	The selection of a market that will be the most advantageous segment in which to offer a product or service. Also called a market target.

Tariff	In trade, a tax or fee levied on incoming goods by governments to protect their domestic providers of such goods from cheaper imports. Published list of fares, freight charges, prices, rates, etc.
Tax Implications	Conditions or actions that can affect the amount of taxes payable.
Taxes	A fee levied (charged) by a government on a product, income, or activity.
Ticker	A scrolling display of current or recent security prices and/or volume.
Trademark	A distinctive name, symbol, motto, or design that legally identifies a company or its products and services, and sometimes prevents others from using identical or similar marks.
Trade Secret	A formula, process, system, tool, etc. which provides a company with a competitive advantage.
Trading Company	A company that connects buyers and sellers within the same or different countries but does not typically get involved in the owning or storing of merchandise.
Trading Platform	Software provided by a stock broker in order to buy and sell shares in the stock market.
Trend Analysis	A comparative analysis of a company's financial ratios over time.
Trends	The current general direction of movement for prices or rates. Also, increasingly frequent or widespread behavior.
Underwriting	The procedure by which an underwriter brings a new security issue to the investing public in an offering. In such a case, the underwriter will guarantee a certain price for a certain number of securities to the party that is issuing the security. Thus, the issuer is secure that they will raise a certain minimum from the issue, while the underwriter bears the risk of the issue.
Uniform Resource Locator	A specific character string that constitutes a reference to an Internet resource, usually by its acronym, URL.
United States Copyright Office	The US Government body that maintains records of copyright registration in the United States.

United States Patent and Trademark Office	An agency in the United States Department of Commerce that issues patents to inventors and businesses for their inventions, and trademark registration for product and intellectual property identification.
URL	Acronym for Uniform Resource Locator.
USCO	Acronym for United States Copyright Office.
USPTO	Acronym for United States Patent and Trademark Office.
Variable Expense	A cost of labor, material or overhead that changes according to the change in the volume of production units. Combined with fixed costs, variable costs make up the total cost of production. Also called variable cost.
Venture Capitalist	An investor who engages in venture capital projects. Venture capitalists seek opportunities involving businesses that are growing or are in risky market segments, since these businesses generally have a harder time obtaining loans. Frequently called VCs.
Virtual Private Network	A secure, resilient, scalable voice and/or data network created over present circuits using tunneling technique.
Virtual Receptionist	An outsourced call-handling person trained to manage your calls exactly as an in-house employee would, but from another location.
Voice-Over Internet Protocol	Commonly refers to the communication protocols, technologies, methodologies, and transmission techniques involved in the delivery of voice communications and multimedia sessions over Internet Protocol (IP) networks, such as the World Wide Web.
VOIP	Acronym for Voice-Over Internet Protocol.
VPN	Acronym for Virtual Private Network.
Web Analytics	The measurement, accumulation, analysis and reporting of Internet data for purposes of understanding and optimizing web usage.
Web-Based	Of, relating to, or using the World Wide Web.
Web-Based Business	A company that does most of its business on the Internet, usually through a website that uses the popular top-level domain, *.com*. Also called an Internet business, web business, dot-com company, or simply a dot-com.

Web Hosting	A type of Internet service that allows individuals and organizations to make their website accessible via the World Wide Web.
Webmaster	A person responsible for maintaining one or many websites. Also called a web architect, web developer, site author, or website administrator.
Wholesale	The purchase of goods in quantity for resale purposes. Also called wholesale distribution.
Wholesale Distribution	See *wholesale*.
Working Capital	Current liabilities subtracted from current assets. Working capital measures the liquid assets a company has available to build its business.
World Trade Organization	Presently the only global international organization dealing with the rules of trade between nations.
WTO	Acronym for World Trade Organization.

Resources

ExpertBusinessAdvice.com

At **ExpertBusinessAdvice.com**, our goal is to become your complete resource for simple, easy-to-use business information and resources. Enjoy reading about techniques and processes necessary to develop and grow your business. **ExpertBusinessAdvice. com** offers an array of tools and resources to help you along the way by offering tutorials, downloadable templates, real-life examples, and customer support. You can even email us and a qualified member of our staff (yes, a real person!) will review your inquiry and get back to you. Now you can take charge of your professional growth and development, learn from others' success, and make a dramatic positive impact on your business. Learn the principles and practices that seasoned professionals use, at **ExpertBusinessAdvice.com,** for free!

THE WAY FORWARD BEGINS HERE...

Want to learn how to start a business? Are you looking for an additional income stream? No problem—we can get you started down the right path. Do you want to know how to plan, creating the necessary documents to obtain financing for your business? Maybe you just want to learn how experienced business leaders streamline financial models, maximize output, inspire managers, and incentivize employees, tapping the full range of resources available. Regardless of your needs, **ExpertBusinessAdvice. com** is here for you!

www.expertbusinessadvice.com

CRASH COURSE for ENTREPRENEURS

Many novice entrepreneurs have little more than a brilliant idea and a pocketful of ambition. They want to know *Now what?* This 12-title series tells *exactly what you must know*, in simple terms, using real-world examples. Each two-hour read walks you through a key aspect of being an entrepreneur and gives practical, seasoned, reader-friendly advice.

Whether your dream business is dog walking or high-tech invention, home-based or web-based, these books will save you time and trouble as you set up and run your new company. Collectively, these three young Florida-based serial entrepreneurs have successfully started seventeen new companies across a broad range of sectors and frameworks, including finance, international sourcing, medical products, innovative dot-com initiatives, and traditional brick-and-mortar companies.

A Crash Course for Entrepreneurs—From Expert Business Advice

Starting a Business – Everything you need to build a new business, starting from scratch.

Sales and Marketing – Solid guidance on successfully developing and promoting your business and its brand.

Managing Your Business – Proven techniques in managing employees and guiding your business in the right direction.

Business Finance Basics – Tax tips, funding resources, money management, basic accounting, and more!

Business Law Basics – A must-know overview on types of businesses, risks and liabilities, required documents, regulatory requirements, and the role of a business attorney. *Co-Author: Mark R. Moon, Esq.*

International Business Basics – A solid read covering the key issues and actions you must consider to succeed in doing business abroad. How to choose a target market, define opportunities and risks, fund and grow it, and make your global business thrive.

Business Plan Basics – The quality of thinking and planning in your business plan is critical to your start-up's success. Learn how to build a great one and see samples of excellence.

Time and Efficiency – Wheel-spinning is the most destructive force in business. Make the most of your time to maximize income and motivate employees.

Franchising – A how-to guide for buying and running a franchise business.

Supplemental Income – Can't commit full time? No problem! Here's how to make extra money in your spare time.

Social Media – This rapidly-growing networking and advertising medium is changing the world. Here's how to use it to grow your business.

Web-Based Business – The biggest, most valuable companies out there today are Internet businesses. Here's why, and how you can build one yourself.

Paperback and eBook format available. 160 or 192 pages, 6 ½" × 9" (16.5 × 23 cm), US$18.95, with extensive glossary and index.

expertbusinessadvice.com   moonlawgroup.com   novavistapub.com

Index

Tip: We suggest you check the Glossary for definitions related to items in this Index.

About the Authors

Scott L. Girard, Jr.

Editor-in-Chief, Expert Business Advice, LLC
Email: scott@expertbusinessadvice.com

Before joining Expert Business Advice, Scott was Executive Vice President of Pinpoint Holdings Group, Inc., where he directed multiple marketing and advertising initiatives. Scott was a key player for the Group, negotiating and facilitating the sourcing logistics for the commercial lighting industry division, which supplied clients such as Gaylord Palms, Ritz Carlton, Marriott, Mohegan Sun, and Isle of Capri with large-scale lighting solutions. His vision and work were also pivotal in the growth and development of Bracemasters International, LLC.

Scott has degrees in Business Administration and English Writing and is a published contributor to various periodicals on the topics of economics and politics. He is also a co-author and series editor of A Crash Course for Entrepreneurs book series. A graduate of the United States Army Officer Candidate School and the Infantry Officer Basic Course, Scott is a combat veteran, having served in Iraq, Afghanistan, Kuwait and Qatar in support of Operation Iraqi Freedom, Operation Enduring Freedom, and Operation New Dawn.

Originally from Glendale, California, Scott now lives in St. Petersburg, Florida with his wife and son. Scott is a regular contributor to www.expertbusinessadvice.com. His side projects include a collection of short stories and scripts for two feature films. His motto: "Words have meaning."

Michael F. O'Keefe

Chief Executive Officer, Expert Business Advice, LLC
Email: mike@expertbusinessadvice.com

In 2004, Michael founded O'Keefe Motor Sports, Inc. (OMS Superstore), eventually growing it into one of the largest databases of aftermarket automotive components available on the web. Currently, aside from his position at Expert Business Advice, LLC, Michael is the President of Pinpoint Holdings Group, Inc. and the Vice President of Marketing for Bracemasters International, LLC.

At Pinpoint Holdings Group, Inc., Michael focuses on strategically building a diverse portfolio of assets including technology, biomedical and traditional brick-and-mortar companies, as well as commercial and residential real estate. He also played a key role in facilitating the logistics of the commercial lighting branch of the company, bridging the gap between Pinpoint's office in Wuxi, China, and their commercial clients.

Recently, Michael's passion and talents for contemporary business techniques and practices were demonstrated in the exponential growth of Bracemasters International, LLC. Michael developed dynamic marketing campaigns, web-based marketing strategies, and e-Commerce initiatives resulting in Bracemasters' website viewership growing by 17,000 percent in just under two years and its annual revenues growing by over 100 percent. Michael's talent, leadership ability, and prospective vision make him a vital player in the contemporary business arena.

Michael holds degrees in both international business and real estate with a focus on commercial real estate development and finance. He credits over 20 years of competitive sailing with his father as the reason for his tactical and highly strategic approach to business structure, growth strategy, and leadership.

Originally from Delavan, Wisconsin, Michael now resides in Orlando, Florida.

Marc A. Price

Director of Operations, Expert Business Advice, LLC
Email: marc@expertbusinessadvice.com

Marc has collaborated with the Federal Government, United States Military, major nonprofit organizations, and some of the largest corporations in America, developing and implementing new products, services and educational programs. Equally skilled in Business-to-Business and Business-to-Consumer functions, Marc has facilitated product positioning, branding and outreach efforts on many different platforms for the organizations he has worked with.

As an entrepreneur, Marc has successfully directed the launch of seven different companies, ranging from traditional brick-and-mortar establishments to innovative dot-com initiatives. Four were entertainment production companies (sound, lighting, staging, logistics, talent, entertainment), one was a business services company serving small companies, one was concerned with business and land acquisition, and two were website and business consulting services. Using his expertise in organizational management and small business development, Marc's latest focus is on working with new entrepreneurs and small-to-medium-sized businesses in emerging industries.

As an accomplished public speaker and writer, Marc has appeared on nationally syndicated television and radio networks, in national print publications, and has been the subject of numerous interviews and special-interest stories. Marc is a regular contributor to www.expertbusinessadvice.com.

Marc received his Bachelor of Science in Organizational Management from Ashford University. He and his wife divide time between Orlando, Florida and elsewhere, including an active schedule of international travel. His motto: "You can't build a reputation on what you are going to do."—Henry Ford

Mark R. Moon, Esq.

Email: MMoon@MoonLawGroup.com
Founder and Managing Attorney, Moon Law Group, P.L.

In 2009, Mark founded the Moon Law Group. His vision was to provide effective and educational legal services to individuals and small businesses by using technology and general business knowledge to create a new model of legal practice that is accessible and affordable to the average person and small business owner. Prior to founding the Moon Law Group, Mark was associate counsel in a large law firm specializing in the representation of banking institutions through their business and real estate operations in both state and federal jurisdictions. Before attending law school, Mark founded and operated a real estate sales and technology company. He also worked in the financial services sector, managing a branch location and earning his NASD series 6 and 7, Florida Real Estate, and Life, Health and Annuity licenses.

Mark earned his Bachelor of Science from the Warrington College of Business at the University of Florida, with Honors, majoring in Finance with a minor in Economics. He graduated from the Levin College of Law at the University of Florida, earning certificates in Estates, Trusts, Family and Elder law. Mark is currently admitted to practice in the State of Florida, the US District Courts of Florida and the US Court of Veterans' Appeals. He is a veteran of the US Army and Operation Iraqi Freedom. Mark is a graduate of multiple military and business leadership courses.

Originally from Madeira Beach, Florida, Mark now lives in St. Petersburg, Florida with his wife and three children. His other work includes the growth of his firm, veteran-focused charity work and the advancement of the collaborative practice of law. His motto: "There is a problem: What are the solutions?"

Kate Scribner

Email: info@novavistapub.com
Writer and Entrepreneur

Kate Scribner's international experience began when she was 16, living for a year with an American Field Service host family in São Paulo, Brazil. After passing her doctoral oral exam in literature and teaching writing at the University of Minnesota, in the US, she left academic life and went into publishing.

Kate worked for years as an editorial director, marketing director, and international business development director at various publishing houses. Later she became Vice President International in a global training and consulting company, leaving the US to live abroad. In 2002 she founded her own publishing company, selling international rights and distributing her list around the world. In the course of her career she's written articles on hunting and fishing, a book on customer service, and a volume of fiction for children, as well as translating others. She lives in Belgium and spends a good deal of time traveling worldwide for business and fun.

Business Efficiency Resources

Get More Done Seminars

Grooms Consulting Group, a sister company to Nova Vista Publishing, offers proven training that saves professionals one month or more of time wasted on email, information and meeting inefficiency.

• 83% of all professionals are overloaded by email – we can save up to 3 weeks a year, per person
• 92% want to improve their information storage system – we can make searches 25% faster and more successful
• 43% of all meeting time is wasted – we can save up to another 3 weeks per year, per person

"We saved 15 days a year!"
Matt Koch, Director of Productivity
Capital One Financial Services

Three Two-Hour Modules: We offer three powerful seminars: **Get Control of Email**, **Get Control of Info**, and **Get Control of Meetings**.
They can be delivered in any combination you wish and can be customized.
Who Should Attend? Anyone who handles email, stores information, and attends meetings. Leaders leverage their position for added impact.
Delivery Options: Seminar, keynote speech, webinar, e-learning, and executive coaching.
Return on Investment (ROI): We can measure the impact of every session on participants with five-minute online pre- and post-surveys. We deliver a report that shows time saved, productivity gained, participant satisfaction, and other significant impacts.

Special pricing is available for groups.

Three *Get More Done* Modules: Combine and Customize as You Wish

1. GET CONTROL OF EMAIL
• Pump up your productivity by eliminating unnecessary email
• De-clutter your jammed inbox
• Write more effective messages
• Discover time-saving Outlook® / Lotus® tech tips
• Improve email etiquette and reduce legal liability
• Choose the best communication tool

2. GET CONTROL OF INFORMATION
• Get organized, once and for all
• Never lose a document again
• File and find your information in a flash; make shared drives productive
• Make better decisions with the right information
• Create an ordered, stress-free folder structure throughout your system

3. GET CONTROL OF MEETINGS
• Meet less and do more through virtual and other advanced options
• Reduce costs, boost productivity and go green with improved, efficient virtual meetings
• Run engaging, productive live meetings
• Discover time-saving e-calendar tips
• Keep every meeting productive and on track, make follow-ups easy

Satisfaction Guaranteed
We guarantee that the vast majority of your people will rate our seminars "excellent" or "good", or your money back.

"A huge hit with our people!"
Joel Burkholder
Regional Program Coordinator – ACLCP

Contact: Kathe Grooms
kgrooms@groomsgroup.com